Poems Past and Present

A Guide for AQA GCSE English Literature (8702)

About the Author

After graduating from Oxford University with a degree in English Language and Literature, and 26 years working for British Airways, I decided to train as a teacher of English. For the next ten years, I taught in the secondary state sector in a multi-cultural and socio-economically diverse area west of London. On my retirement in 2016, I was second in the English department, co-ordinator of the A Level English Literature curriculum and Lead Year 13 tutor, co-ordinating university entrance applications. I am also an Examiner for AQA GCSE English Literature.

My approach to studying poetry is straightforward: unless you understand *what is happening* in the poem – the event, incident or story – about which the poet weaves his literary magic, there can be no understanding of a poet's literary techniques. The two are inextricably intertwined. There is a LOT of very variable analysis of poetry on the internet. Much of it stems from a failure to understand *what is happening*. This failure leads to students having a rattle-bag of literary terminology but with nothing on which to hang it. Naming metric forms and rhyme schemes, and poetic techniques with no understanding of why the poet has used them, is a waste of time. It also leads to spurious, and erroneous, analysis of structure and form. I have read, in exam papers, that the *"shape of the line on the page, if you turn it sideways, corresponds to the furrows of a field."* Or, *"the varied line length suggests the outline of the Manhattan skyline"*. Students do not come up with ideas like this unless there is a fundamental failure to grasp the links between *substance* (the *"what is happening"*) and *structure* (rhythm and rhyme) and *language* (the words used).

This guide is an attempt to make these links and help students appreciate why a poem has been written in the way that it has.

Contents

About this Guide

The Guide has been written primarily for students of GCSE English Literature as specified by AQA in the post-2015 syllabus (8702). It addresses specifically the requirement **to study one cluster of poems** taken from the AQA poetry anthology: *Past and Present: poetry anthology* and the requirement **to analyse and compare Unseen Poetry**. These requirements are assessed in Paper 2 (Modern Texts and Poetry) Section B: Poetry and Section C: Unseen poetry, of the examination.

The Guide covers all the poems in both the *Love and Relationships* and the *Power and Conflict* clusters in the Anthology.

The Guide aims to address Assessment Objectives AO1, AO2 and AO3 for the examination of this component, namely:

AO1: Read, understand and respond to texts. Students should be able to:
- maintain a critical style and develop an informed personal response
- use textual references, including quotations, to support and illustrate interpretations. *

AO2: Analyse the language, form and structure used by a writer to create meanings and effects, using relevant subject terminology where appropriate.

AO3: Show understanding of the relationships between texts and the contexts in which they were written.

*Whilst there is no specific mention of "*making comparisons*" as part of AO1, the mark scheme makes it clear that the examiners expect the essay response to be "comparative", described as "*Critical, exploratory comparison*" at the highest band.

The poems are explored individually, and links and connections between them are drawn as appropriate. The format of each exploration is similar:

- A summary of the key themes of the poems, with a note on possible connections and links to other poems in the cluster
- An explanation of key features of the poem that require contextual knowledge or illustration and the relationship between the text and its context.
- A brief summary of the metric form, rhyme scheme or other structural features
- A "walk-through" (or explication) of the poem, ensuring that what is happening in the poem is understood, how the rhythm and rhyme contribute to meaning, an explanation of the meaning of words which may be unfamiliar, an exploration of language and imagery and a comment on main themes.

A note on "relevant subject terminology" (AO1)

This means the use of the *semantic field* of literary criticism – or "jargon". Criticism has a language to describe the features peculiar to the study of literature, just as football has words to describe manoeuvres and equipment – *"penalty"*, *"off-side"*, *"wing"*, *"long cross"*, *"throw-in"*. To be able to critique literature, you need to know this language and use it correctly. Throughout this guide, literary terminology has been *italicised*, indicating that these words need to become part of your vocabulary when discussing the texts and writing essays. For illustration, here are some very basic literary terms that are often carelessly used and will lose you marks in the exams if you do not apply them correctly.

Text – is the printed words. The *whole text* is all the words that are identified, usually by a *title*, as belonging together as an integral piece of writing.

A *Book* is a collection of printed pages bound together to make a *whole text*. A *book* can be any text – fiction, non-fiction; play, novel; car maintenance manual, encyclopaedia. A *book* is a **physical** entity, like "*DVD*" or "*scroll*", not a creative one.

A *novel* is a particular kind of text – a *genre*. It is characterised by certain creative features, such as being *fictional,* usually *narrative in structure* and with various *characters* who do things, or have things happen to them. It may be *descriptive*, and may contain *dialogue.*

A *novella* is a short novel. Its scope and the number of characters are often (but not always) more limited than in a novel.

A *short story* is a narrative fiction, of variable, but limited length.

A *play* is another *genre*. It is designed to be performed and watched, rather than read. It can be *fictional* or *non-fictional*, or a mixture. It is predominantly made up of *dialogue* between *characters*, although there may be descriptive elements within this *dialogue* and in the *stage directions*.

A *poem* is a particular *genre* which is characterised by the deliberate, and recurring, use of *rhythm* and *rhyme* and/or by a particular attention to *diction*, in the form of *word-choice* and *imagery*. It is opposed to *prose*. However, there are *poetical* prose writers whose language uses the distinctive features of poetry – such as *alliteration*, *rhythm* and *imagery*.

Beyond these simple definitions, there are a host of other literary terms. These terms have been used where they are necessary to describe features of the texts and are defined on the first usage, and subsequently when repeated, depending on how common the usage and the relevance to the poem under discussion.

A note on "critical comparisons" (AO1)

The new specification refers to *"links and connections"* as well as *"comparisons"* between literary texts. There is little to be gained from making, often spurious, comparisons which fail to illuminate the text, and structuring essays which say: *"on the one hand/ on the other"*. The highest band marks challenge the student to be able to *synthesise* their knowledge of the texts – a higher level skill. The Mark Scheme refers to: *"critical, exploratory, well-structured comparison"*. Further guidance on this is given in the section on *"Links and Connections"*.

A note on "create meanings and effects" (AO2)

There are very few marks to be gained by simply spotting and correctly naming literary techniques. Comments on literary techniques **must** be linked to purpose and meaning to gain marks in the higher bands. This principle has been followed in the analyses of the texts. See the section *"About the Author"* for a further comment on the dangers of spotting literary techniques in isolation from the meaning of the text. Not all literary techniques used are discussed in the commentaries; only those that are particularly relevant to the discussion of meaning, form or theme have been explored.

You are also required to know something about *metric form* – the use of rhythm and the terms which are used to describe it – and relate the use of *metre* to meaning. In the commentaries, stressed beats are in **bold** and the *metric feet* are shown with the / symbol. *"A Note on Metre"* has been given at the end of this guide, which explains the main metric forms used, with examples.

A note on "relationship between texts and context" (AO3)

There is a requirement to have some knowledge of the biographical, social-economic, political or literary context in which these poems were written **and show how this is reflected in the text.** Understanding of meaning is enriched by knowing relevant autobiographical details, particularly where the subject matter focuses on relationships. Many of the poems use allusions and references to classical mythology, the Bible, popular culture and general knowledge, without which meaning is obscure and appreciation limited. Relevant contextual information has been given for each poem in either the introduction under "**Context**" or in the analyses. Where poets appear in both clusters, relevant contextual information has been repeated, on the basis that most students will only read their chosen cluster.

AO3 also refers to "*ideas*". By this is meant "*the contexts in which texts are engaged with by different audiences, taking the reader outside the text in order to inform understanding of the meanings being conveyed.*" This is a long-winded way of saying that you need to show some grasp of the wider implications of the text; what are the ideas about how we live our lives that the poet is presenting? For example, in "*Bayonet Charge*" and "*Charge of the Light Brigade*", it might be the idea of blind patriotism which drives men to fight even when afraid. Comments could be made on whether and how this "idea" persists in modern warfare.

A note on *typography*

Remember – most poems, until relatively recently, were written by hand and therefore the look of a poem on the page when it is printed is not necessarily an indication of intent by the poet – it may be the *typography*. *Typography* is the way the words of the poems are printed on the page. There are conventions in *typography* for poems which are adhered to by certain editions but ignored in others. For example, many of the pre-1900 poems start each line with a capital letter. This is of no significance – it is a typographical choice. Similarly, whether lines are indented or blocked may be typographical, rather than meaningful. Similarly, line length is often a feature of *metre*. Check that a line is, in fact, "longer" metrically before commenting on it. You should always look for other, supporting, evidence if you are going to make any link between layout on the page and meaning.

Capitalisation of individual words in a poem may be deliberate. Pre-1900 poets often capitalised virtues, as in Truth, Beauty, Purity or Nature. You should be able to tell whether capitalisation is a printing convention, or for a purpose, from the context.

You will see in the older poems that the final *"-ed"* of the past tense of verbs may be depicted as *"'d"*, as in *"Volley'd and thunder'd"* in *"The Charge of the Light Brigade"*. This is simply to indicate that the words should be pronounced as two syllables. Sometimes, to make a full metric line, they would have been pronounced as three: *"thun-der-ed"*.

A note on "themes"

The question in the examination for *Paper 2 (Modern Texts and Poetry) Sections B: Poetry* will ask for a response to a central concern or idea which may form the focus of the poem or be an integral part of its meaning. You will be asked to explore the presentation of this *"theme"* in one named poem and one other poem of your choice.

Section C: Unseen Poetry will ask you to explore the presentation of a given *"theme"* in an Unseen poem and then link it to the treatment of the same or similar *theme* in a second Unseen poem.

These "themes" could include, but not be limited to: an **emotion** – such as love, loss, sorrow, joy; the **evocation of "place"**, as the subject of the poem, or as the setting for the poem; the treatment of **abstract concepts** such as Time, Power, Death, or Religion; a **"happening"** such as War, Childhood, Marriage; types of **relationships between men and women, such as** loving, unsatisfactory, jealous, obsessive, changing. The range is very broad.

Where a poem from the anthology lends itself to suggesting a particular theme, this has been noted in the overview and linked to other poems which have similar themes. However, these suggestions are illustrative, not exhaustive; one of the skills to be mastered is to know the texts well enough to be able to link them to themes which may not be immediately obvious. Students should spend some time mapping the links between poems thematically and illustrating how these themes are treated in similar or differing ways.

As well as links of *theme,* links and connections can be made between *narrative voice, form, structure* and *language*. At the end of this book are some questions which should be considered when making links and connections, and when analysing the Unseen. (See *"Links and Connections."*)

Preparing for the Unseen Poem

The best preparation for this component of the examination is to read, and listen to, poetry, of all kinds, regularly. There are a number of websites which will deliver a *"poem-a-day"* to your mobile. These two combine contemporary American poetry with classics:

https://www.poets.org/poetsorg/poem-day
https://www.poetryfoundation.org/newsletter

The Poetry Foundation website enables you to browse poems clustered by theme. This is a particularly useful feature to enable you to practise comparing poems.

How to use this Guide

As the modern poems within the anthology are copyrighted to the authors, it has not been possible to print them within this Guide. You will therefore need to read the commentaries with a copy of the text alongside. However, the poems have been quoted in places for illustrative purposes. Where the poems are out of copyright, they have been quoted at greater length.

Bibliography

AQA have published a guide to *"Teaching Context"* which is available to teachers. Further reading on context can be found on the following useful websites:

http://www.bl.uk/romantics-and-victorians/articles/the-romantics#

www.victorianweb.org

Many of the modern poets have their own websites, which are worth exploring for autobiographical details and commentaries on their poems.

Love and Relationships

Introduction to the Romantic Poets

There is one thing that *any fule kno*[1] about the "Big Five" Romantic poets – they died in reverse order of being born. So, Wordsworth (1770 – 1850), Coleridge (1772 – 1834), Byron (1788-1824) Shelley (1792 – 1822), Keats (1795 – 1821).

The Romantic movement, or Romanticism, was a reaction to the preceding Age of Enlightenment, which had valued rational, scientific thought, above the revelation of emotions, the imagination, and the transforming power of the natural world. Wordsworth, in his preface to *"The Lyrical Ballads"* (1798), which he co-authored with Coleridge, described poetry as the *"spontaneous overflow of powerful feelings"*. Romantic Poetry is characterised by a *focus on the sensibilities:* a recognition of the *"sublime"* in the natural world; a willingness to engage in the imaginative possibilities of a supernatural world which co-exists with ours; the expression of intense emotions; a questioning of the nature of Art and aesthetics and the creative process; an exploration of spirituality, religious beliefs and the meaning of life. *Medievalism* and *Gothic* are sub-genres of Romanticism. *Medievalism* harks back to the legends of King Arthur and the Knights of the Round Table, and the conventions of chivalry and courtly love, with idealised relationships between men and women. *Medievalism* provides the setting for the *Gothic*, but in *Gothic* the focus is on the supernatural and the relationships between men and women are often highly eroticised. The poets were also revolutionary in their support for the overthrow of the established order through non-violent protest and championed the plight of the working poor.

The poets were also anxious to break away from the rigid rules of *poesy*, such as the strict use of rhythm and rhyme, exhibited by earlier poets such as Alexander Pope (1688 – 1744), seeking

---

[1] Molesworth in *"Down with Skool"* (sic), G. Willans. 1953.

for a more natural rhythm, closer to speech, and a more colloquial *lexis*.[2] However, many of their earlier poems are written in prescribed forms – such as *sonnets* – and their poems often do have a regular rhythm and a regular rhyme scheme.

In this cluster, although only the first two poems are by "Romantic" poets (Byron and Shelley), many of the others share characteristics with them, particularly in their **evocation of the natural world, the landscape and the weather,** using this as a backdrop, and commentary on, the relationships which are the subject of the poems. This may be through the use of *pathetic fallacy*[3], as in Browning's *"Porphyria's Lover"*, or Hardy's *"Neutral Tones"*, or in looking to Nature as a model for human behaviour, as in Sheers' *"Winter Swans"* or Barrett Browning's *"Sonnet 29"*.

---

[2] *Lexis* is vocabulary
[3] *Pathetic fallacy*, literally *"false feeling"*, is to reflect human emotions in the weather or landscape; so, it rains when people are crying or sad.

When We Two Parted – Lord Byron

Context

Byron was notorious for his love-life. He was described by one of his early mistresses, Lady Caroline Lamb, as *"mad, bad and dangerous to know"*. He is the origin of the *"Byronic Hero"*, a sexually alluring but dangerous, brooding and essentially ego-centrical male protagonist who re-occurs through much of later Victorian fiction, including Rochester in *"Jane Eyre"* and Heathcliff in *"Wuthering Heights"* by the Brontes. From the age of 28, until his death eight years later, Byron lived abroad, following a scandal involving a possible incestuous relationship with his half-sister which resulted in the birth of a child, and the breakdown of his marriage. He died in self-imposed exile in Missolonghi, Greece.

The poem was written in 1816 and is generally considered to refer to Byron's earlier affair with Lady Frances Wedderburn Webster, who later had a scandalous relationship with the Duke of Wellington (the *wellington boot* is named after him), who defeated Napoleon at the Battle of Waterloo in 1815.

Themes

This is a poem about a secret, and doomed, love-affair. The poet shows his **disappointment in love** and **sense of betrayal.** To a modern reader, it can also be seen as an example of the **differing attitudes to men's and women's sexuality** that existed throughout the 19th century. Byron laments his lover's infidelity and the shame he feels on discovering that she has had multiple partners. However, he seems not to reflect on his own behaviour, although Byron was a notorious womaniser. It is an extremely self-indulgent and self-obsessed reaction, illustrative of the double-standards of the time. The theme of **male sexual obsession** is shared with *"Love's Philosophy"*, *"Porphyria's Lover"*, and *"The Farmer's Bride"*. Barrett Browning shows a similar intense focus on the object of her desire in *"Sonnet 29"*. *"Singh Song"* reflects male desire, but with humour and with a clear recognition of the autonomy of the woman and a more equal treatment of male and female sexuality, which might be expected of contemporary poetry in reflecting modern society.

Form, Structure and Language

The poem is highly structured with four stanzas of *octets*[4] with a regular rhythm and rhyme scheme. This reflects the poet's obsession with his lover and his nagging sense of betrayal, even though they parted some time before. The poem is written predominantly in *dimetres* – two strong beats, or *stresses*, in a line, with an occasional *trimetre* (three stresses in a line). There is considerable variation in the value of the *metric feet*[5]. This gives the lines a more natural rhythm, closer to speech – which is appropriate as the poet is addressing his ex-lover. However, the regular beat and the repeated *"silence and tears"*, suggest a note of melancholy, like a funereal drumbeat, as the poet continues to feel the pain of his disappointment. The regular rhyme scheme – *ababcdcd* – adds to the insistent tone.

The poem opens with the poet (and we can assume it is Byron – he was notorious for his *affaires*) recalling the moment when he and his lover first parted – some years before the events of the poem. The refrain *"in silence and tears"* is established as characterising their doomed relationship. When they parted, they are only *"half broken-hearted"*, which could refer to both of them, but may refer to just Byron. However, the characterisation of the woman as *"pale"* and *"cold"* is reflective of her feelings for him, which are dying, and foretell their final separation and her infidelity.

---

[4] An *octet* is eight lines
[5] A *metric foot* is a combination of light and heavy beats. So, an *iamb* is a metric foot made up of one light and one heavy stress (ti-**TUM**). See the section *"Rhythm in English Verse"* at the end.

The second stanza moves between *then* - when *"the dew of the morning"* of their parting feels cold, as prescient of how he feels now - and *now,* when he hears news of her. *"light is thy fame"* means that she is being gossiped about, because of her love affairs, as does the *"they name thee"* of stanza 3, suggesting pointing fingers and whispered slanders. He *"shares in her shame"* because he has been her lover; he is worried about tarnishing his reputation by association with her.

However, stanza three reveals that no-one has made the connection between them; even so, he *shudders* to think of his former feelings for her, as if they have become tainted by her later infidelities and by the risk to his reputation. He seems to regret that at least as much as the loss of love.

In the final stanza, he wonders how he would react were they to meet in person again. Their former liaison was clearly clandestine: *"in secret we met"*. He is keeping it secret still and bewails that she seems to have forgotten about him. The poem ends on the refrain, showing his on-going regret and sorrow, imagining that the emotions he felt, when they parted may years before, would still well up in him.

Love's Philosophy – Percy Bysshe Shelley

Context

If the name "Shelley" is familiar, but not the poet, this is because it was his second wife, Mary Wollstonecraft Shelley, who wrote the Gothic novel *"Frankenstein"*, whilst on holiday in Geneva with Shelley, Byron and John Polidori, who wrote the early vampire novel, *"The Vampyre"*. Shelley and his circle were unconventional, if not scandalous, for their time, but were well-connected and wealthy, and could largely afford to ignore public and private criticism, although they were at times estranged from their families. They believed in the supremacy of the individual spirit over convention and rules, indulging in multiple relationships and declaring their atheism.

Shelley's short life was remarkable, not just for the poetry, but for the drama. He was expelled from Oxford for declaring his Atheism; eloped, at nineteen, with the 16-year-old Harriet Westbrook; ran away two years later with Mary Godwin, the 16-year-old daughter of Mary Wollstonecraft, a noted writer on female emancipation, and William Godwin, a noted philosopher; had children by both Mary and Harriet within three months of each other in 1814/15; travelled with Mary and her sister, Claire, to Switzerland with Byron, who was having an affair with Claire; married Mary two months after his first wife, Harriet, was found drowned in the Serpentine, heavily pregnant; he drowned in a boating accident in Italy aged 29.

Themes

This is a **poem of seduction**, allied to the *"carpe diem"* school of poetry, where a man encourages his lover to give in to his demands. It is in the tradition of Herrick's *"Gather ye Rosebuds While ye May"* or Marvell's *"To His Coy Mistress"* (both 17th century). Shelley's argument is that *"mingling"* is part of Nature's natural order, so men and women should follow her example. In fact, if sexual relationships between men and women are to be denied, then what is the purpose of the world? The poem is clearly an expression of Shelley's own "philosophy", his beliefs on how the world should work, and he lived his life accordingly.

Although less obsessive, this poem has similarities in its **focus on male desire** with *"Porphyria's Lover"* and *"The Farmer's Bride"*, although it is *lyric⁶ poem*, rather than a *dramatic monologue⁷*. In the use **of naturalistic imagery**, it is aligned to Elizabeth Barrett Browning's *"Sonnet 29"*, to *"Porphyria's Lover"* and *"Neutral Tones"*.

Form, Structure and Language

Like *"When We Two Parted"*, the poem is highly structured, with the same *abacdcd* rhyme scheme and use of stanzas of *octets*. Like Byron's repetition of *"silence and tears"*, Shelley also uses repetition of words or phrases, such as *"mingle"*, *"kiss"* and the question at the end of each stanza. The structure of Shelley's poem is similar to a *canzonetta* – a lyric form used in Italian poetry, by which he may have been influenced, as the poem was written in 1820, when Shelley was living in Italy. Shelley's lines are predominantly *tetrametres*, which gives it a more leisurely, less insistent tone than Byron's poem, although his approach to the object of his desire is similarly self-serving. The light eroticism of the poem is enhanced by the mix of "*masculine*" and "*feminine*" line endings. A "*masculine*" ending is where the stress falls on the last syllable of the line; a

---

⁶ A *lyric* poem was originally a song accompanied by a lyre. It is now used to describe a (mainly) non-narrative poem that expresses strong thoughts and feelings.

⁷ A *dramatic monologue* is a poem where the voice of the narrator is not the poet's. The poet creates a distinctly different *persona* who addresses the reader.

"feminine" one where the line ends on an unstressed syllable. So, the masculine endings in the first stanza are *"Ocean"* *"emotion"*, *"divine"*, *"thine"* and the feminine endings are *"river"*, *"ever"*, *"single"*, *"mingle"*.[8]

Shelley uses the natural landscape as an *analogy* for the sexual union of men and women, citing a series of examples where geological features can be shown to *"mingle"*, *"mix"*, *"clasp"*, and *"kiss"* one another in an orgy of *pathetic fallacy*[9]. In the first stanza, Shelley draws on the process of springs (*"fountains"*), becoming rivers which run into the Oceans. He suggests that this is ordained by a higher power than him in the use of *"winds of Heaven"*, with its archaic capitalisation, and the *"law divine"* in line 6. As an atheist, Shelley is not referring to a Judaeo-Christian deity, but rather to a power embodied by Nature, more in the classical tradition, although it remains unspecified. Having apparently proven his point, he asks why he and his sweetheart cannot be like these natural processes and *"mingle"* their beings?

The second stanza opens with a more insistent command to *"See"* as he points out further examples of unions in nature, the *"mingling"* now giving way to the more intimate and overtly physical *"clasp"* and *"kiss"*. The *repetition* of *"kiss"* and *"clasp"* and the *anaphora*[10] of the opening *"And"* in lines 11, 13 and 14 increases the urgency of the tone. The final question suggests that this union in nature is worth nothing, unless they follow nature's example. After all, they are the children of nature and should be governed by the same laws.

---

[8]http://www.bl.uk/learning/langlit/poetryperformance/shelley/poem2/shelley2.html - Aviva Dautch

[9] *Pathetic fallacy* – literally, *false feeling* – suggests the landscape, or weather, or other natural phenomena reflect, human emotions.

[10] *Anaphora* is a rhetorical device that uses repetition at the beginning of a clause for effect. The *"I have a dream"* speech of Martin Luther King is a famous example of the use of *anaphora*.

Porphyria's Lover – Robert Browning

Context

This is arguably the greatest poem in the whole cluster. Browning is the master of the *dramatic monologue*, the poet against which all other poets who write in this form are judged. Browning's *"My Last Duchess"*, another *dramatic monologue*, is in the *Power and Conflict* cluster, which you may like to read for comparison. A *dramatic monologue* is a poem where the poet takes on a *persona* - a character who is not himself - and speaks in his voice. However, that is not to say that the poet is entirely absent. The poet may refer to emotions, events or ideas which he has himself experienced, or be using the *persona* to debate topical questions of the day.

Browning delighted in exploring the minds of socio- and psychopaths: in other poems by him, the Duke in *"My Last Duchess"* is a murderer; the woman in *"The Laboratory"* is planning to poison at least three of her rivals in love; the man in this poem strangles his lover with her own hair. His poems are often set in historical time periods; he also wrote *dramatic monologues* in the *personae* of Renaissance artists of the 14th century, such as Andrea del Sarto and Fillipo Lippi. This poem, however, is set in a contemporary, Victorian setting.

The name *"Porphyria"* means *"purple"* in Greek. It has nothing to do with the disease of the same name (which has led some commentators into errors of interpretation). The poem was written in 1836 and the disease not named until more than 50 years later. The name infers that the woman is of a superior social class to the man, as purple is often associated with royalty or high birth. There is a contrast between the *"cottage"*, in which the man lives, and the *"gay feast"* which she abandons to be with him. Her Lover also refers to freeing herself from *"pride"* to be with him, suggesting that she has to stoop to his level, and to *"vainer ties"*, commitments to a relationship which satisfies her need for status, but not passion.

Themes

The Victorian poets used the *dramatic monologue* to **debate the position of women in society, sexual relationships** and gender identity, the nature of work and finding purpose in life, religious doubt and **societal ills**, in their search to make sense of their lives in a world that was rapidly changing. The *dramatic monologue* allowed them the freedom to explore radical ideas without the fear of public censure. They were not always successful - commentators of the day sometimes saw through the pretence and criticised them as scandalous.

In this poem, Browning seems at least as interested in the psychology of an individual man (the *"Lover"*), as in society in general. The theme of **male sexual obsession** is shared with *"When We Two Parted"*, *"Love's Philosophy"*, and, particularly, *"The Farmer's Bride"*, which is also a *dramatic monologue*. The Lover of the title is a psychopath, sexually possessive and murderously jealous. Like Byron, he exhibits **a sense of betrayal**, as the woman has a husband (or another lover). To a modern reader, it can also be seen as an example of the **differing attitudes to men's and women's sexuality** that existed throughout the 19th century in main stream society.

Form, Structure and Language

Poetry is an oral art form. It is the poet's voice - heard through the rhythm, the rhyme, *syntax* and punctuation, as well as the auditory poetic techniques - which lifts the words off the page and makes sense of them. To understand a *dramatic monologue*, you have to HEAR the voice. With the *dramatic monologue*, and Browning's in particular, you have to be sensitive to what the *persona* is NOT saying, as much as to what he IS saying. We hear Browning's views on his subject, and his subject matter, in the gaps. The technique which he uses most to create the cadence of the voice of the *persona* and reveals what he is actually like, as opposed to the version of himself that he gives the listener, is *enjambment* - running the sense of a line onto the next (giving emphasis to the first words of the succeeding line) and *caesura* - breaking or stopping in the middle of the line.

In this poem, Browning also uses the rhythm and rhyme scheme to create the disconnect between what the speaker says, and what he does. The poem is written as one long stanza, in fairly regular *iambic tetrametres[11]*, but is formed of English *quintains[12]* with a regular rhyme scheme of *ababb, cdcdd* .... The unbalanced rhyme scheme suggests the mentality of the man, whilst the regular rhythm and rhyme keep the whole under tight control. However deranged he might be, the *persona* maintains an air of calm rationality. Browning plays with this form by sometimes using the five lines to present complete images or actions; at others, he runs them together to move the narrative forward, or to create startling juxtapositions to show that the man has lost his grasp of reality.

In the first four lines, Browning uses *pathetic fallacy* to reflect the state of mind of the speaker – *"sullen"*, *"spiteful"* and *"vexed"* at Porphyria's refusal to give herself only to him – and to foreshadow the dramatic events to come: *"The sullen wind was soon awake, / It tore the elm-tops down for spite"*. It is essentially *"spite"* that drives him to kill Porphyria, as he cannot bear sharing her. The rhyme scheme and rhythm further reflect his madness. Browning establishes the regular *iambic tetrametre* in the first four lines, in order to create the anticipation of a regular metre throughout. The break in metre at line five - *'I listened with heart fit to break'* - from four stressed syllables to five, reflects how the *persona* is broken.

---

[11] *Iambic tetrametre* is a line with four stressed beats in a metric pattern of *iambs*, one light stress followed by a heavy stress (ti-**TUM**). See the section on Metre at the end of the Guide for a full explanation.

[12] A *quintain* (or *quintet*) is a five-line stanza. An *English quintain* has the rhyming scheme *ababb*.

The man describes Porphyria as if she were a dutiful wife, shutting the door and making up the fire, reflecting Victorian men's expectations of women. Victorian women in the mid-19th century had few rights; their purpose was to serve their husbands, look after the home and bear his children; they were largely dependent on men for financial support. Porphyria is portrayed as doing all that is associated with the dutiful female, as well as giving sexual favours: *'She put my arm about her waist, /And made her smooth white shoulder bare'*.

It is notable how the *persona* sits and watches Porphyria, without responding to her: *"no voice replied"*. She has to resort to overt sexual advances to break through his *"sullen"* silence. The description of her making advances to him is an instance of how Browning uses the *quintain* to present a single image – from *"She put her arm..."* (line 16) to *"her yellow hair."* (line 20).

The next 10 lines appear to give Porphyria's explanation of why she has come to him, but it is filtered through the prism of the man's jealousy. She *"murmurs"* that she loves him – but this is followed by the man's judgement of her action, in the *"she/Too weak"*, where Browning uses the *enjambment* to emphasise the *"Too weak"*. It is his interpretation of her motivation and action that we hear in his sneering *"too weak"*, *"struggling"*, *"pride"* *"vainer ties"*, *"give herself to me"*. He is commenting on her being torn between her position as a wife (her *"pride"*), and her duties to her husband (the *"vainer ties"*), and her desire to be with him. The rhyming of *"dissever"* and *"forever"* tells us what he wants – all of her, all to himself.

The next *quintain* shows how Browning uses the form to surprise and reveal character, breaking the regular rhythm with the successive use of *enjambment* and *caesura* in *"at last I knew/Porphyria worshipped me."*, and *"surprise/Made my heart swell"*. The jaunty rhyming of *"still it grew"* and *"what to do"* marks the point at which his psyche moves from jealous lover to murderer. Jealous of the time spent with another, the speaker's solution is to kill her so that she can *'Give herself to (him) forever"* and he can complete his possession of her: *'That moment she was mine, mine fair·'*. This shows the Lover's desire to both possess and dominate, even if, in possessing, he destroys her. Browning this time links the two *quintains* at lines 40 and 41 with *"And"*, and uses the *caesura* in line 41 to create the shock of the matter-of-fact *"And strangled her"*.

The poem then moves into the realm of horror, as the Lover seems to wind the clock back, restoring Porphyria to the life he has just taken. His self-justification in the repeated she felt *"no pain"*, is followed by the revelation that the Lover forces open Porphyria's eyes, describing them as still laughing, with no tears. He then *"untightens"* the tress about her neck, which brings the blood back to her cheek, which he ardently kisses. He then props her head up on his shoulder, in an awful parody of her actions when she came to him. Notice the use of *enjambment*, again, across the *quintain* of lines 50/51: *"my shoulder bore/Her head"*, to shock. Throughout, Browning likens Porphyria to a flower; in the contrasting delicacy of the image of the bee in a flower bud for her closed eyes; the drooping head like a dead flower on a stalk; the *"rosy"* head. This heightens the macabre of the scene. The extent of his psychosis is made clear in his assertion that she is *"smiling"* and *"glad"* that she has now left her former distractions behind and had her *"darling one wish"* – that she has *"gained"* her Lover *"instead"*.

The final *quintain* is split in two, with the first two lines completing the Lover's self-satisfied reflection on her happiness and the third bridging to the final couplet, where he makes his final pronouncement: *"And all night long we have not stirred, /And yet God has not said a word!"* The Lover feels no guilt for his actions because, he claims, God has not passed judgement. *"Porphyria's Lover"* demonstrates the ultimate objectification of women, the poem's overall message being *'If I can't have her, then no one can'*.

By revealing the mania of the lover and subjecting him to ridicule, Browning shows that he is highly critical of this view of the relationships between men and women and the double standards to which women are subjected. In this, his attitude can be contrasted with Byron's in "*When We Two Parted*". The reasons can perhaps be found in the contrast between the two men's relationships with women in their lives. Browning courted Elizabeth Barrett, who was older than him and in poor health, for two years before finally eloping with her to escape her father's refusal to allow her to marry anybody. She was already an established poet and he encouraged her writing, in part sacrificing his own creative impulse. On the other hand, there is Byron, the serial womaniser and self-imposed exile whose life was characterised by betrayal and scandal.

Sonnet 29 – "I think of thee!" – Elizabeth Barrett Browning

Context

The unlikely love-affair, and marriage, of Elizabeth Barrett and Robert Browning is one of the great love stories of the Victorian age. Always in frail health, Elizabeth lived her early adult life sheltered by a domineering father, her mother having died when Elizabeth was 22, in 1828. After 1840, devastated by the death of her two brothers, Elizabeth was largely confined to her house, writing her poetry and letters. She published in journals and, in 1844, a two-volume collection of her poetry was published on both sides of the Atlantic, heralding her as one of the foremost poets of her day. The two volumes reached the house of Robert Browning, himself a published poet, but struggling to establish himself. The two began to write to each other, a correspondence, and courtship, which lasted for two years before they eloped in 1846 to escape the disapproval of Elizabeth's father. They moved to Italy, where they stayed until Elizabeth's death in 1861.

"*Sonnets from the Portuguese*", from which this Sonnet is taken, were written during the period of Robert's courtship and are love poems written about her experience of falling and being in love and are often addressed to Robert himself.

Themes

This is an erotic love poem which celebrates Elizabeth's strong **emotional, intellectual and physical attraction** to Robert Browning. In contrast to the poems of Byron and Shelley, it is inclusive of the object of her desire, the focus being on their union, and it also ends positively, on the promise of a consummation, rather than the bitter aftertaste of Byron's or Hardy's love affair, or the frustration of Shelley's or Mew's longing. This poem, Sheers' *"Winter Swans"* and Nagra's *"Singh Song!"* and Dooley's *"Letters…"* are the most **positive representations of relationships** between men and women in the cluster. However, Barrett's poem is also obsessive in its image of longing for surrender to the object of her desire.

Form, Language and Structure

The poem is a *Petrarchan sonnet* - 14 lines of *iambic pentametre* with a regular rhyme scheme *abbaabba* (*octet*[13]) *cdecde* (*sestet*[14]) . Petrarch was the prime exponent of the sonnet form in Italy in the 14th century but it was adopted in England by Shakespeare and others, although sometimes with a different rhyme scheme.

Sonnets are traditionally love poems, although modern sonnets can cover any kind of experience. They usually put forward some kind of argument or premise - an idea for discussion - in the *octet* which is answered or countered in the *sestet*, although this "answer" can occur at any point, even as late as the final two lines. This switch in the argument, or answer to the question, is called the *volta,* or *"turn".*

The central image is of Elizabeth as a wild vine twisting herself around the trunk of a tree, which is Robert Browning. In the first *quatrain,* (the first four lines) the *"vine"* is her thoughts of him when he is absent. Line 5 is effectively the *volta* and the next four lines recognise that his presence is better than her thoughts of him and she pleads him to come to her. The *sestet* declares how she will abandon herself to him and that her thoughts will be overcome by the nearness of his physical presence.

---

[13]An *octet* is eight lines
[14] A *sestet* is six lines

In the opening quatrain, the poet's thoughts of her lover are likened to *"wild vines"* – a plant which has vigorous growth and can grow around its host tree, completely smothering it, so that there is *"nought to see"* except its own greenery. The object of her desire is completely consumed by her longing.

The next four lines (lines 5 to 8) introduce a caution – the *"Yet"* warns that he must not think that her thoughts are enough for her; his physical presence is so much *"better"*. She pleads for him to *"Renew [his] presence"* – come back to her again, as a lover *"should"*.

When he does, his presence will drive all thoughts from her head; her thoughts will *"Drop heavily down"* as if they were vines falling from the trunk of the tree as it *"Rustles [its] boughs"*. She will not be able to think about him any more – she is overwhelmed by his physical presence: *"I am too near thee"*.

The imagery is highly erotic, the *"trunk all bare"* clearly phallic, the words *"Drop heavily down"* showing her surrender to his physical presence and *"burst, shattered, everywhere"* strongly suggestive of orgasm. The Victorians are often stereotyped as prudish and straight-laced. This poem, like *"Porphyria's Lover"* and *"Love's Philosophy"*, suggest otherwise.

Neutral Tones – Thomas Hardy

Context

Hardy is probably better known for his novels than for his poetry. He wrote poems in his youth, but he did not return to writing poetry until the completion of his last novel, "*Jude the Obscure*", in 1895. His novels, particularly "*Tess of the D'Ubervilles*" and "*Jude the Obscure*", are acknowledged as some of the best novels of the era, challenging Victorian bourgeois values, exploring the plight of women and Victorian sexual hypocrisy, and the effects of the Industrial Revolution on the rural poor.

Hardy's relationships with women were problematical. He had a number of disappointing romantic relationships as a young man; his first marriage, to Emma Gifford, ended unhappily, with a long separation, although he was devastated by her death and she is the focus of much of his later poetry; he was for some years enamoured of a married woman who would not have an affair with him, but remained a life-long friend and correspondent; in his later life, he was infatuated with a succession of much younger women. Two years after his first wife's death, he remarried, but the marriage was not happy.

This poem is from his early period, written when he was twenty-seven, but not published until 1898 in the collection "*Wessex Poems*." Hardy had just returned from London, where he studied and practised as an architect until becoming a full-time writer. One of his briefs was the removal of gravestones from the old St Pancras cemetery to make way for building a railway into London. They can still be seen stacked up against an old ash tree, whose roots now grow around them. It is known as "*The Hardy Tree*". It may be this that inspired the setting for this poem.

Themes

Like Byron's *"When We Two Parted"*, the poem reveals Hardy's feelings of **disappointment in love** and **sense of betrayal** at a failed relationship. It too centres on the memory of the parting between the lovers, with the woman falling out of love with the man and the man's feelings of bitter regret. Like Byron, Hardy recalls the look of his former lover – her eyes, her smile – and relates these to his surroundings, which are uniformly grey and lifeless, reflecting her indifference to him and his numbed response. The poem can be contrasted with Sheers' *"Winter Swans"*, which also recounts a meeting of two lovers, in winter, by water. However, Sheers sees in the two swans on the lake, that *"mate for life"*, an image of reconciliation and a future that is full of promise.

Form, Language and Structure

The negative moods of Hardy and his former lover are also reflected in the regularity of the verse form. The poem is written in four stanzas of *quatrains* (four lines), of *tetrametres* – four stressed beats in a line. It uses *enclosed rhyme*[15], *abba,* the circular rhyme scheme adding to the tone of hopelessness.

"Neutral Tones" is a pun on the greyness of the setting and the woman's neutrality towards him, as she has grown bored with the relationship. Like Browning, he uses *pathetic fallacy* in the lifelessness of the setting: the *"white"*, colourless, lifeless, sun, abandoned by a loving God[16]; the *"few leaves"* which are *"grey"* rather than a living green; the *"starving"* ground, which bears no fruit or flower.

The woman's boredom is conveyed in the *"eyes that rove"*, looking for another object of greater interest than the man in

---

[15] *"enclosed rhyme"* is a rhyme scheme that has the outer lines of a stanza rhyming with each other and the inner ones rhyming with each other.

[16] *"chidden"* means *"cursed"*. It is an archaic form of the past tense of the verb *"to chide"*.

front of her, whom she has lost interest in. They speak to each other, but their words lack conviction: they "play" "to and fro" like a game, going through the motions of arguing about which of them was most hurt by the relationship.

The image of the dead smile on the woman's mouth is both complex and striking, in the use of *paradox*[17]. The first line of the stanza reads as if it will conclude that the "*deadest thing*" in this landscape is her smile. But instead, it becomes the only thing in the landscape "*alive enough*" to die; everything else - the sun, the leaves, the ground, her eyes - are even more dead. But this smile has the strength "*to die*" – to turn from a "*smile*" to a "*grin*", like on a corpse, leaving everything equally bleak. It also foreshadows worse to come – like a bird of ill-omen, perhaps foretelling his future unhappiness.

The poet concludes that, from that day, every bad experience with love that he has, recalls this parting – the look on her face, the cold sun, the grey tree with its dead grey leaves and the pond. She has become the model for all his unhappy experiences.

---

[17] *Paradox* is an apparent contradiction – here between "dead" and "alive", as the smile is both at the same time.

Letters from Yorkshire – Maura Dooley

Context

Maura Dooley is an educator and currently teaches Creative Writing at Goldsmith's College, London. She went to the University of York and has taught at the Arvon Foundation in Yorkshire, a centre for teaching creative writing. Much of Dooley's poetry is autobiographical, and we can assume that *"Letters from Yorkshire"* recalls an important friendship in her life, maybe made during her time spent in that county.

Themes

The poem is a gentle reflection on **a positive relationship** and can be contrasted with the poems of Byron and Hardy, which both recall broken relationships.

The poem reflects on **how relationships can be sustained at a distance**. Communication is a recurring theme in Dooley's poetry. Dooley's poem is full of **contrasts:** between a rural and an urban way of life; between working on the land and working at a desk; between communicating by letter and by computer. However, at the end, **the two lives come together** as they both watch the television – a broadcast communication medium which, like the radio, can reach many people simultaneously, enabling them to share experiences. Sheers' poem *"Winter Swans"* similarly begins in separation and ends on an image of two people united, in the two lovers holding hands. Barrett Browning's *"Sonnet 29"* is also a love poem written to someone who is absent and is resolved by the image of the lovers united, breathing in the same air.

The poem has similarities with Heaney's *"Follower"*, which also explores contrasting lifestyles, in this case the life of Heaney's father as a farmer and Heaney's life as a writer. However, in Heaney's poem, there is no "coming together"; rather, Heaney asserts the validity of his own choice of career almost defiantly.

Form, Structure and Language

The poem is written in *free verse,* with no regular rhythm or rhyme, although each stanza has three lines of similar length. The poet creates a forward momentum by using *participles* (verb endings in *-ing*) - *"digging"*, *"planting"*, *"breaking"*, *"clearing"*, *"pouring"* - to vividly describe her friend going about his work. She also uses *enjambment* to link lines and stanzas together, as between *"singing/as"*, *"season/turning"*, *"you/who"*, her thoughts tumbling from her as she describes their separate, busy lives. This movement is in contrast to the final moment when they come together in front of the television, as their *"souls tap out messages"* and they are united and at rest.

It is not evident in the first stanza that the man described is well known to Dooley, as she writes of him in the third person, *"he"*. However, he breaks off his work, *"digging"* and *"planting"*, to write to her about the *"lapwings"* (birds that return to arable land to breed) which suggests that the relationship is important to him, as he wishes to share these first signs of Spring with her. Their closeness is also evident in her imagining how his *"knuckles"* tingle as they warm up indoors. She seems to be drawing on memory here.

She confirms the specialness of their relationship by denying it – *"It's not romance, simply how things are"* - as if to convince us, but in so doing, she suggests the opposite. There are many real-life and literary instances of "romances" carried out by letter, where people become fond of each other without meeting. The romance between Robert Browning and Elizabeth Barrett started with a correspondence; another is documented in *"84, Charing Cross Road"* (1970) which tells of a real twenty-year correspondence between Helen Hanff, an American, and the owner of a bookstore in London; the film *"You've Got Mail"* (1998), starring Tom Hanks and Meg Ryan, based on the play *"She Loves Me"*, written in the 1930s, is a fictitious example. Dooley's assertion is also undermined by the switch to the second person, and more intimate, *"You out there,"* which makes the poem one side of a conversation addressed to the writer in Yorkshire.

She contrasts his outdoor life, in tune with nature, with her own, as a writer sitting at a *"blank"* computer screen, which is lifeless. There is a gentle irony in the alliterative phrase *"heartful of headlines"*. *"Heartful"* suggests powerful, truthful emotions; *"headlines"* are designed to capture attention, are often *clichés* or puns and short-lived. She also *"feeds words"* into the computer, the *personification* of *"feeds"* suggesting it is a hungry animal, like the public who read her copy. The *rhetorical question "Is your life more real?"* summarises how she feels about the contrast between their two worlds.

In the fourth stanza, the poet imagines how her friend in Yorkshire would respond to this question. She suggests that he does not see his life as particular or special, although very different from hers, as he grapples with the effects of the weather.

However, the *metaphor "pouring"* conveys his eagerness to share his world with her, and also his generosity, as he has stopped going about his tasks to write to her. Notice the emphasis given to the *metaphor* of *"pouring"* by the use of the *enjambment* across the stanza and the naturalistic image of *"air and light"* to contrast with her artificially lit room.

This correspondence between them connects them imaginatively and emotionally, so much so that she describes their *"souls"* being linked, so they can communicate with each other when they are sharing the same activity, watching television, even though they are separated by distance. The *"icy miles"* is a reminder that the weather her friend is grappling with in the north links them, as they share the same winter, even if her experience of it is very different.

The Farmer's Bride – Charlotte Mew

Context

Charlotte Mew lived a long and troubled life, touched by tragedy and ending in suicide. She was the eldest of seven children: three brothers died in childhood and two were committed to mental institutions in their twenties. She and her sister vowed never to marry to avoid having children who might be similarly affected. This dark personal story forms the subject of much of her poetry. She herself became increasingly reclusive in later life, following the death of her sister, and was admitted to a nursing home suffering from delusions in 1928, where she took her own life by drinking disinfectant.

She did not write a large body of poetry. This is probably her most famous work, and the title piece of her first published volume. Its publication in 1912 made her a literary, although not financial, success and she was noticed by both Thomas Hardy and Virginia Woolf. Although the date of composition is not known, it seems to hark back to the Victorian era in its depiction of country life. However, in its examination of the relationship between the Farmer and his young bride, and the frank depiction of his sexual frustration, it looks forward to the Modernist movement of the early 20th century.

Themes

The poem explores **an unhappy, and unhealthy, relationship** between a farmer and his young bride, whom he has married to cure his own loneliness and sexual frustration. It explores **the position of women in society and their sexual relationships with men**. This is not an unusual theme in Victorian literature, although rarely expressed so graphically, and may well have been the aspect of the poem that attracted Hardy, who explored women's sexuality in a number of his novels. In showing **male sexual obsession** and **male pride** it is similar to Byron's "*When We Two Parted*" and Browning's "*Porphyria's*

Lover", where the desire to possess the woman overwhelms any concern for her own wishes. Aspects of the poem also suggest that there is a strong **mythological** element to the story; it is a tale of the real world and the land of faery, or myth, interacting.

Form, Structure and Language

Like *"Porphyria's Lover"*, the poem is a *dramatic monologue*, with a male *persona* who tells his story. He is characterised by the use of *dialect* words and phrases which show his social class and his rural life and occupation. Although the object of his desire is silent, she is vividly depicted by likening her to various animals and aligning her with the natural, and the imagined, worlds.

The poem is written in *common or ballad metre*, with four stressed beats to a line, mainly of *iambs (ti-TUM)*. This, coupled with the use of *dialect*, give it an archaic feel – a sense that this is an old tale being told. Indeed, there is more than a suggestion that the *"bride"* is an enchanted being – not human, but *"fay"*.

There is a regular, and complex, rhyme scheme in each stanza, although it varies between stanzas. Mew uses the rhyme to at times join, and at others separate, her sequence of images and the stages in the story. So, in stanza one, the story opens with an account of the marriage, contained within the rhyme scheme *"maid /do /woo /afraid"* (abba) and moves on to the next idea of her fear of him with a new scheme *"human /day /woman /fay /away."* However, the two schemes are linked by the *enjambment* between *"afraid/Of love"* which moves the story onwards.

There is also a sequence of seasons over which the narrative takes place, although spread over three years. He weds in Summer, she runs away in Fall and the climax of the poem takes place in a cold Winter.

The Farmer's frustration at his lonely and celibate lifestyle and the youth of his chosen bride is made clear in the first stanza. He acknowledges that she is *"too young maybe"* to be married, but he is impatient, and too busy, to take account of her feelings and wishes. He has to marry in the summer, when there is less to do in the fields, and before harvest, his busiest time. So, the wedding takes place with little time for them to get to know each other. The fourth line glosses over the time between the marriage and the situation he now finds himself in, three years later, although the *enjambment* of *"turned afraid/Of love"* and the *euphemism*[18] *"love"* for *"sex"* make it clear that it is their sexual relationship which has frightened her. She turns her back on, not just her husband, but *"all things human"*, suggesting her affinity with a supernatural or fairy world. The farmer's use of naturalistic imagery, which forms part of his *idiolect*[19], is seen here in describing the loss of her smile as the *"shut of a winter's day"*, when night falls early. His *dialect* is used in the form of the past tense of *to run, "runned"*, instead of *"ran"*.

The Farmer's plight is obviously common knowledge in the village, as the neighbours report back to him where she is: *"Out 'mong the sheep"* and it seems to be their comment that she should be in bed (by implication, with him). It is clear that she no longer sleeps in his bed, as he would know she was missing, and he has to check that she is not in the house. So, his male pride (and by inference, the pride of all the men in the village) is being attacked by her refusing to sleep with him, which might explain his actions. The shock that not just the Farmer, but the men of the village, turn out to hunt her down is conveyed in the delayed positioning of the verb *"We chased her..."* after the long subordinate clause at the beginning of line 14, and following the *enjambment* of *"the down"*. Mew shows the men's determination to capture the girl in her use of *parallelism*[20],

---

[18] A *euphemism* is a word substituted for another to make it less harsh, as in saying *"passed away"* for *"died"*.

[19] *Idiolect* is the unique speech pattern of an individual

[20] *Parallelism* is the use of repeated grammatical structures for effect.

using enjambment between lines 17/18 and starting line 18 with *"We caught her,"*. The finality of the farmer locking her up so she cannot flee again is conveyed in the *rhyming couplet* [21]th at ends the stanza: *"last/fast"*.

This stanza also develops the idea of the girl as an other-worldly being, in likening her to a *"hare"* with her *"brown stare"* and her running. A hare, an animal like a large rabbit and with prominent brown eyes, is associated with shape-shifting and the world of the *"fay"* in popular folktales.

In the next stanza, the narrative has moved to the present, indicated by the use of the present tense: *"She does the work..."*. We learn that the girl does her wifely duties around the house, but will have nothing to do with humans, content in the company of *"birds and rabbits"*. Women, but not men, can come close to her; they note how she can calm the farm animals. However, she does not speak to him. The final *quatrain* describes the girl in a series of *simile* s of the natural world: as a *"leveret"*, a young hare; a young *"larch"* tree, which is a deciduous conifer; as sweet spring *violets*. All these are images of youth and the repeated *"wild"* emphasises that, so far, he has been unable to "tame" her. His bewilderment and frustration is conveyed in the rhetorical question *"But what to me?"* It is not enough for him to simply look at her, although he recognises her youthful beauty; he wants more in their relationship.

The penultimate, intensely descriptive, stanza uses a series of images of the coming winter to convey the farmer's feelings of loneliness and abandonment in this loveless marriage: brown leaves on the oak trees; smoke from fires; a lone leaf and a single feather on the icy ground; the holy berries ripening. This last image of them *"reddening"* is also suggestive of the *"ripeness"* of the girl, which means ready to have children,

---

[21] A *rhyming couplet* is two lines that end with a full rhyme.

confirmed by the reference the farmer makes to his desire to have children: *"Some other in the house than we!"*

This idea leads into the final *quatrain* where his sexual frustration is given a voice, helped by the faster rhythm of the first two lines, which are insistently *iambic*. The girl still sleeps separately from him; the word *"maid"* could mean that she is still a virgin or could just be another word for *"young girl"*. He is intensely aware of her presence; there is *"but a stair"* between them, which, it Is implied, he could climb very quickly. This idea is given by the use of the enjambment between *"stair/Betwixt"*, showing how easily this short distance can be overcome. This thought leads to the exclamation of his longing: *"Oh! My God!"*. He recalls intimate details of her: the hair on her arms and its softness; her brown skin; her brown eyes and her long brown hair. All his frustration and longing are poured out in the *repetition* of the two final lines: *"down"* is repeated twice, *"brown"* twice, and then *"hair"* twice.

The reader is left with an uneasy, queasy feeling that the *"stair"* between them might indeed be insufficient to keep him from her and that Mew wishes us to contemplate the possibility of an impending rape.

Walking Away – Cecil Day-Lewis

Context

If the name Day-Lewis seems familiar, that may be because Cecil Day-Lewis is the father of the actor, Daniel Day-Lewis, three times Best Actor Oscar winner, most recently for his eponymous role as "*Lincoln*" in 2012. Cecil Day-Lewis was not only Poet Laureate[22] from 1968-1972, but was a well-known writer of detective fiction, under the pseudonym "Nicholas Blake".

This poem is autobiographical and is written to the poet's first-born son, Sean, by Day-Lewis's first marriage to the daughter of a schoolteacher. The poem was written in 1957 when Sean was twenty-five, making him seven when this football match took place.

Themes

This poem, and the next five in the cluster (as well as the last) explore various **relationships between parents and children**. In this poem, the predominant feeling is one of **loss** as the child grows up and moves out of the close-knit family circle. The poem imagines **the ties that bind parents and children together** and shows the tension between the realisation that the parent has to "let go" of the child if it is to thrive, and the pain of coming to terms with the inevitable emotional and physical distance between them. The poem has a number of images of this parting: "*a satellite/Wrenched from its orbit*"; a "*half-fledged thing set free*"; a "*winged seed loosened from its parent stem*". However, it ends on a positive note and something learned – that it is the loving thing to do to allow the child to find its own path in life. The final two lines have

---

[22] *Poet Laureate* is a public appointment, in the gift of the monarch, which requires the holder to write poetry for certain state and national occasions

become very famous and are often quoted as encapsulating the dilemma facing all parents everywhere.

The poem is written from the point of view of the parent; in this it is unique in the cluster, as the other poems on a similar theme are written from the point of view of the child. However, the ideas are also clearly present in the imagery used by Armitage in "*Mother, any distance…*", where the ties between son and mother are contained in images of a tape-measure and a kite-string, or in the photograph of Duffy's "*Before You Were Mine*" or the memories of Causley in "*Eden Rock*" and Heaney in "*Follower*".

Form, Structure and Language

The poem is addressed to the now-adult son, in a measured and reflective tone which appears to flow freely from one idea to another as he recalls the central incident and then draws meaning from it. However, it is in fact highly structured with a subtle use of predominantly *iambic tetrametre* – four-beat lines of *iambs* (ti-TUM). The flow is created by the use of *enjambment* between lines and across stanzas, and by the rhyme scheme, where the first, third and fifth lines rhyme but lines two and four do not, softening it.

The poem opens with the poet precisely setting the time period of his son's first football match (probably at his new Preparatory school) eighteen years before. It may be that his son reaching 25 is seen as another significant milestone in their lives together, and prompted the poem. The first stanza is notable for the precision with which Day-Lewis details the exact time that this incident took place: it is "*eighteen years ago*"; it is "*sunny*" and the beginning of autumn as the leaves are "*just turning*"; the "*touch lines*" are "*new-ruled*" indicating that it is the beginning of the Autumn term; it is the end of the match. This precise placing of the memory in time and place is similar to Causley's picturing of his parents on the picnic in "*Eden Rock*". Day-Lewis delays the moment that forms the focus of his reflection – the moment the son walks away from him *"towards the school."* It is the moment when the father realises that he is no longer the centre of his son's world; the boy no longer "orbits" his father. This image is similar to Armitage's in *"Mother…"*, where he likens himself to an astronaut taking a space-walk, tethered by a life-line to the mother-ship. The use of the word *"wrenched"*, meaning to pull violently, shows the emotional impact of the sight on the father and the relentless tug of this new environment, and of growing up. The *enjambment* between stanzas one and two mirrors the action of the son *"drifting"* away as the sense "drifts" across the stanza.

The second stanza switches the focus to the son, who seems little and lost entering this new universe: he is *"half-fledged"* like a baby bird that has left the nest too early; he is pathless, no longer having guidance from his parent.

The idea of the boy drifting continues in the third stanza with the word *"eddying"*. An eddy is a small whirlpool in a stream, suggesting the boy's hesitancy and lack of direction. This is continued in the image of the loosed *"winged seed"*. Winged seeds, as from a sycamore, spiral down to the ground and are aerodynamically designed to catch the wind and travel distances. These images represent to the father something that he finds hard to put into words, the *"give-and-take"* of nature which holds both pleasure and pain, as in giving children to parents and then having them taken away as they grow up. The word *"scorching"* shows that these moments leave a painful and lasting impression, and bring one's life into sharp focus: *"irresolute clay"* suggests that, usually, people just go through life without being "fired" up by many things.

The final stanza articulates his learning from this apparently small event – the memory of it still *"gnaws"* at his mind and will not go away. Similarly, the image of Heaney's father in *"Follower"* *"will not go away"*. The memory is seared into his soul. He struggles to articulate his feelings, suggesting that only God could properly express what he is trying to say. God gave his only son, Jesus, to Man and then watched him die. "*Self-hood*" means becoming your own person, as the poet's son will have to do, and as Jesus did, and the "*letting go*" by the parent, as God gave his son, is what has to happen to enable his son to achieve his full potential. The final two lines gain their impact from *parallelism*, using the same grammatical structure in each half of the compound sentence: "*How selfhood/And love*" and "*walking away/letting go*" and by the assertion of the underlying rhythm.

Eden Rock – Charles Causley

Context

Charles Causley is perhaps better known as a writer of poetry for children, although he made no distinction. For someone who was writing alongside Ted Hughes, his close friend, Stephen Spender, Philip Larkin and other modern poets, his poetry seems perhaps old-fashioned, harking back to an earlier age. He is particularly fond of the *ballad* form. His work was popular, but has not been as highly regarded as that of his contemporaries.

Causley was born, and lived most of his life, in Cornwall. His father died, when Causley was seven, of tuberculosis arising from injuries received in the First World War. In the poem, his father is remembered at the age of *"twenty-five"*, the probable age of his death. Causley joined the Navy for the Second World War, but otherwise led a secluded life, for six years nursing his terminally ill mother.

Themes

The poem is an *elegy,* a poem mourning the death of his parents. The main them is of **Loss,** specifically the loss of parents through death. Like Armitage's *"Mother..."*, Duffy's *"Before You Were Mine"* and Heaney's *"Follower"*, the poem is written from the point of view of the adult **child reflecting on his/her relationship with a parent**. In common with Armitage's and Duffy's poems, parent and child are linked at a moment in time, which they recall fondly, but not without an awareness of an inevitable parting. The title of the poem also suggests themes of **loss of innocence**.

Form, Structure and Language

The poem is written with a loose rhythm, but Causley uses *half-rhymes*[23], particularly in the second and fourth lines of each stanza, to knit the lines together. The final line of the poem is isolated to give emphasis to his declaration of how hard he has found the death of his parents.

Child and parents are linked by a memory of a picnic at *"Eden Rock"*, a fictitious place, the name suggestive of the paradise of the Garden of Eden and the loss of innocence which leads to Adam and Eve's expulsion from it. The whole poem can be seen as a *metaphor* for Causley's separation from his parents by death. The idea of the parents *"waiting"* in the first stanza refers to them waiting for him on the other bank of a river that they have crossed to prepare the picnic, and being metaphorically on the other side of life, symbolised by the river, the River Styx over which the souls of the dead were rowed in Greek mythology.

The recollection of his mother and father when they were young and he was a child is detailed and affectionate, as well as clear sighted. It is similar in this to Day-Lewis's memory of the day his son begins to leave him in *"Walking Away"*. They have dressed up in their best clothes for this picnic. The expensive, specialness of his father's suit is indicated by the capitalisation of *"Genuine Irish Tweed"*, a label indicating quality; his mother wears a light summer dress embroidered with flowers (*"sprigged"*) and a straw hat decorated with a ribbon. She has ironed the tablecloth on which the picnic is laid, "keeping up appearances" as she would at home. He remembers her blonde hair, a contrast to the grey it would have been when she died. Note the use of *consonance* to link *"suit/feet"* and *"dress/grass"* in these two stanzas.

---

[23] A *half-rhyme* is where only part of the word rhymes with another, as in *"dress/grass"* in stanza 2.

The details of the Thermos (a flask for keeping drinks hot), the *screw-topped* bottle and the *blue tin cups*, are emblematic of the period between the wars. Like Duffy in *"Before You Were Mine"*, Causley uses cultural icons as a way of fixing memory at a particular place and time. The details are precise and clear, as if captured in a photograph, helped by the use of the full rhyme on *"screw/blue"*.

The *metaphor* is signalled, in stanza four, by the image of the sky being lit by *"three suns"*, symbolic of the three of them, against which his mother *"shades her eyes"* as if looking out from the white light that is said to herald on-coming death. She is looking for her son, who has not yet *"crossed the river"* where his father spins a stone; metaphorically, the child is alive, whilst they are dead. However, the single word *"Leisurely"* is ominous in its positioning alone at the end of the line. In this remembered life, leisure is something this man does not have; he is soon to die.

At first, *"Leisurely"* appears to stand alone in meaning as well, but is linked to the next stanza using *enjambment*. They call to him to join them across the river, showing him a *"not as hard"* path to reach them. In the metaphor, the parents are unaware that their time together is short and that their son cannot join them easily. The parents encourage him to cross the "river" (of death) while he stands helpless on the far side.

The last line, standing alone, merges the remembered reality and the *metaphor* of life and death. He has not realised, until now, how much their loss has meant to him, his vivid recollection calling them up before them and reopening the pain, and how hard it is for him to contemplate joining them.

Follower – Seamus Heaney

Context

Heaney was born into a Catholic family in County Derry, Northern Ireland, the eldest of nine children, one of whom was killed at the age of four in a car-accident. His father and grandfather were farmers, and a recurring theme in Heaney's poetry is his feeling of guilt that he did not follow in his father's footsteps but became a poet and academic. He attended Queen's University, Belfast, but spent the latter part of his life in Dublin. He is certainly one of the heavy-weight hitters in this collection; one of the finest poets of the 20th century, Nobel Laureate, Oxford Professor of Poetry and winner, in 2006, of the TS Eliot poetry prize. This poem is taken from his first collection, *"Death of a Naturalist"*, which was published in 1966, when Heaney was 27.

This poem, like many of Heaney's, is autobiographical. It evokes a rural way of life in Northern Ireland that had changed little over the centuries, when fields were still ploughed by horses, and farms were handed down from father to son through the generations. Heaney shows his keen observation of nature, his images often striking and aligned to the natural world.

Themes

The title *"Follower"* refers to: the child's efforts to follow his father around the farm, literally "in his footsteps"; the idea that children "follow on" from their parents in the line of inheritance; the poet's choice of whether to follow his father in becoming a farmer; the memory of his father that follows Heaney throughout his life. This is another poem that explores **the relationship between parents and children**, from the point of view of the adult child, like Causley's *"Eden Rock"*, Armitage's *"Mother…"* and Duffy's *"Before You Were Mine"*. Like *"Eden Rock"*, the poem recreates a vivid memory of the poet as a child with his parent, but the memory foreshadows the parting that is to come. In "*Eden Rock*", it is the river that forms the link between the past and the present, whereas here it is the ploughing. Both poems end with the adult drawing a lesson from the memory. In Heaney's poem, the poem ends on a note of **guilt**. Like Causley, Heaney seems to have been unprepared for the effect that the death of his parent would have on him. For Heaney, memory has the power to awaken uncomfortable truths about his relationship with his father.

Form, Structure and Language

The poem is similar to Causley's in its use of *quatrains* and half-rhymes. The poem is highly structured, each stanza being a *quatrain* in *iambic tetrametre* with a regular *abab* rhyme scheme of *full* and *half-rhymes*[24]. However, Heaney is the master of *enjambment*, so that this regular rhyme and rhythm have the sound of natural speech. Heaney also uses *enjambment* to mimic the meaning of the words.

Much of the imagery of the poem likens the ploughed fields to a seascape, in which the farmer is a ship or a sailor. This imagery is used in other poems by Heaney. So, in describing his father in the first stanza, Heaney uses the *metaphor "globed"* for his shoulders, which are rounded and muscular, suggesting his power and his mastery of his world. This is developed into the *simile* of him being a ship at sea with the *"full sail strung"*. The command of the man over the horses is shown by the word *"strained"*, suggesting effort and exertion by the horse, whilst all the man does is *"click"* his tongue.

Heaney's pride in his father is shown in the incomplete sentence *"An expert."* which opens the second stanza, creating a *caesura* to give the words emphasis. Whereas Causley used cultural icons (the *"Tweed"* suit, the *"tin cups"*) to precisely date

---

[24] A *full rhyme* a rhyme where the whole word rhymes with another, as in *"strung/tongue"* in stanza 1. A *half-rhyme* is where only part of the word rhymes with another, as in *"sock/pluck"*

and recreate his memory, Heaney uses the *semantic field*[25] of ploughing to demonstrate the craftsmanship and precision of the actions he describes. The *"wing"* is the broad part of a plough blade which sets the angle; *"sock"* is the blade which pierces the earth. The *"sod"* is the earth, which *"rolls"* over like the parting of waves, cleanly and efficiently.

The second and third stanzas show Heaney's mastery of *enjambment*, using it to *replicate* (copy) the movement of the horses as they plough - up one line of the field, turning at the top, and heading back down the field. The *"headrig"* is the end point of the line of a furrow, where the horses turn to make their return. His father's expertise in turning the horses is conveyed by the *enjambment* across the stanza: *"with a single pluck/Of reins"*, the word *"pluck"* spoken naturally on a rising tone, imitating the movement and "landing" on the *reins*. Similarly, in the next line, although *"round"* syntactically makes sense at the end of the clause, the way one says *"turned **round**"* gives an uplift in the voice, expecting a resolution, which comes in the next line with *"And **back**"*, with the emphasis on "**back**".

Stanzas four and five introduce the image of Heaney as a child copying his father as he follows helplessly behind while he ploughs. The motion of *"Dipping and rising"* again suggests the movement of waves. The child cannot interpret the actions his father takes; he thinks that all he has to do is *"close one eye"* and *"stiffen [his] arm"* to be like him. Heaney acknowledges the legacy his father left him by describing it as a *"broad shadow"*.

In the final stanza, Heaney's realisation that he is unable to follow in his father's footsteps, literally and metaphorically, is conveyed in the use of the listed participles: *"tripping/falling/ Yapping"*. Now, however, the tables are turned. The followed has become the follower, Heaney tied forever to the memory of his father and to the decision he took to become a poet, not a farmer.

---

[25] A *semantic field* is the vocabulary associated with a particular topic

"Mother, any distance" – Simon Armitage

Context

Simon Armitage and Carol Ann Duffy, whose poetry is also in this cluster, are probably the most well-known poets today, partly due to their frequent anthologising by Exam boards, partly as both have public profiles – Armitage was appointed Oxford Professor of Poetry in 2015; Duffy was Poet Laurate between 2009 and 2019. Their poems have similarities: both are often autobiographical; both reference the popular culture of their childhoods and of today; both draw on the literary poetic tradition to give layers of meaning to their poetry; both use a variety of forms and styles, particularly the *dramatic monologue*; both often write in an intimate, conversational style.

Armitage was born, and still lives, in Yorkshire, and remains close to both his parents. After leaving Portsmouth University (then Polytechnic) he spent some years working as a Probation Officer and his early poems reflect the troubled lives of young men. This poem comes from *"Book of Matches"*, published in 1993, one of his earliest collections.

The poem can be assumed to be at least semi-autobiographical, referencing his move to his first house, where he is helped by his mother to measure up for curtains and carpets.

Themes

Another poem on **the relationship between parents and children** and the **inevitability of them growing up and away** from one another. The poem also expresses the feelings of the adult child as he moves out of the family orbit by leaving home; the freedom he will have appears boundless, but also intimidating and not without risk. The poem has similarities with Day-Lewis's *"Walking Away"* but seen from the point of view of the child. In that poem, the man sees that the son is unsure about what the future will bring as the child is *"hesitant, eddying away"*. Here, it is Armitage who does not know whether he will *"fall or fly"*. Day-Lewis ends his poem on the realisation that the love of a parent for a child is shown in the *"letting go"*. Armitage expresses this idea in his image of the mother *"pinching"* the tape measure to the very end until something *"has to give"* and he reaches for his freedom. Both poems have images of the son *"space-walking"* away from the parent, around whom he has orbited during childhood.

Form, Structure and Language

Each of the poems in the first of the three sections of *"Book of Matches"* is written in 14 lines, which would suggest *sonnet form*, and they have been described as *sonnets* by the publisher and by critics. As printed, this poem is unique in the collection in that it appears to be in fifteen lines; however, it is feasible that line 10, in fact, runs to the end of *"has to give"*, which would sustain the rhyme scheme.

Given this, it can be seen that the poem is divided into an *octet* and a *sestet*[26], the *volta*[27] or turn occurring at line 9 where the focus of the poem shifts from the Mother to the son. The *octet* has the rhyme scheme *aabbcccd*. The *sestet* similarly uses *half-rhymes* and a final *rhyming couplet*: *"climb /give /pinch /reach /sky /fly"* to give the rhyme scheme *aabbcc*.

Alternatively, the short "line 11" can be seen as a kind of literary joke, in that the *sonnet form* "gives way" as the Mother and son reach the *"breaking point"*, where they have to separate, the extra line breaking the rhyme scheme and the fourteen-line structure.

---

[26] An *octet* is eight lines and a *sestet* is six lines.

[27] The *volta* is a shift in the subject or argument of a sonnet, or it may be where the answer to an initial question is answered. The *volta* often takes place between lines eight and nine, but can take place anywhere.

The poem uses a number of *metaphors* for the ties between mother and child and their inevitable parting as the son reaches adulthood and moves away, both physically and emotionally. The affection of the son for his Mother, and hers for him, is evident, first in the direct address with which the poem opens, "*Mother*," and secondly in the poignancy of the image of the Mother holding on until the last minute before she sets her son free.

In the first *quatrain*, the son acknowledges his need of his mother's help; he cannot manage the task of starting out in his new life without her support. A "*span*" is usually the distance between the little finger and the thumb on one hand; here it appears to refer to the distance between outstretched arms. If he needs to measure more than this, he needs help. The measuring of the house, using the tape-measure, is used as a *metaphor* for the link between them and their mutual dependency. The "*walls*" and "*floors*" stretch around him, undecorated, vast and bare like a "*prairie*", the unbroken miles of grassland that lay before the first explorers of the American mid-West. His life stretches ahead of him, yet to be explored, and on which he has not made a mark.

The second *quatrain* retains the focus on the mother; she holds the tape at the "*zero end*" signifying "year 0" of his life, when he was born, like an umbilical cord. He carries the tape with him, measuring the house and calling "*back to base*" (his mother) the measurements that he is taking, just as he would tell her of what was happening in his life as he was growing up. But then he is "*leaving*", going up the stairs, the tape still "*spooling*" out behind him, but he is getting more distant from her now as he grows up and as the years grow ("*unreel*") between them. He switches the *metaphor*, seeing himself now as a "*kite*" on the end of a string which is "*anchored*" by his mother on the ground below.

The focus shifts from the mother to the son at the *volta* in line 9. The *sestet* introduces a new set of images. He is now almost free, seeing himself walking in the *"space"* of the upstairs, which he imagines as cosmological space; he is an astronaut "space-walking", but is still tethered, by the "life-line", to the "mother-ship". But once he gets to the attic, the tape-measure/life-line has almost run out. The line between him and his mother is almost at *"breaking-point"*, although she still hangs on him to the last moment (*"last one-hundredth of an inch"*). For him to break free, he has to find a way out – an escape hatch. He reaches for it and sees *"endless"* space – the opportunities the future holds for him. It is up to him now whether he succeeds or fails, alone. Notice that the poem ends with them still tied together, thus leaving his future uncertain, but also acknowledging that they will be forever intertwined.

Before You Were Mine – Carol Ann Duffy

Context

Carol Ann Duffy is the current Poet Laureate, appointed in 2009, the first woman to be appointed to the post. Like her predecessors, Tennyson and Hughes, she also writes for occasions of national importance, as when she commissioned the poetry collection "*Jubilee Lines*" for the Jubilee of the Queen's accession to the throne.

Duffy's poetry is frequently anthologised for students, on the basis, presumably, that being a modern author she is more "accessible" than poets of an earlier age. Unfortunately, this belief is erroneous. Much of Duffy's poetry is autobiographical, reflecting on her childhood, first in Glasgow and later in Stafford, and frequently refers to the popular culture of her youth – the 1950s and 1960s. She assumes significant prior knowledge of this culture, which she uses to enrich her narrative. Similarly, Duffy writes in a strong literary tradition which harkens back to Shakespeare and the 17th century Metaphysical poets. Indeed, much of Duffy's poetry is Metaphysical in its use of *conceit* (a complex metaphor) and in her choice of verse forms, such as the *sonnet*. She also writes *dramatic monologues* in the persona of historical or literary figures, notably "*Salome*", "[Miss] *Havisham*" and "*Anne Hathaway*" which lose much of their meaning without prior knowledge of their stories.

The poem was included in the collection "*Mean Time*" (1993), when her mother was still alive (she died in the early 2000s). Duffy has commented at length on this poem, confirming that it is "*entirely autobiographical*". The full article can be found here and is worth reading for an in-depth commentary on the context and themes, as well as the structure:
http://www.sheerpoetry.co.uk/gcse/carol-ann-duffy/gcse-anthology-poems/before-you-were-mine

Themes

The poem is written from the point of view of the poet as an adult child looking back at her childhood, in this case at a photograph of her mother before the poet was born. In the photograph, the woman is young and carefree, glamorous as a film-star, full of hope and promise. The poem explores **the relationship between parents and children** and, in particular, the realisation, as in *"Eden Rock"*, that they once had **a life independent of their children.** The *"Mine"* of the title suggests the child's **possessiveness**, whereas the adult Duffy appreciates how her mother gave up her previous life with the birth of her daughter. As in Armitage's *"Mother..."*, there is clearly affection between the two. Further exploration of the themes can be found in Duffy's article.

Form, Structure and Language

Duffy has pointed out the overall structure of this *free verse* poem, beginning and ending with a *"pavement"*, in Glasgow where Duffy was born, in stanza one, and Stafford, England, where she mostly grew up, in stanza four. She describes it as a *"collage"* of images of her mother, drawn from the photo and her own memory, growing up. There are many references to popular culture, her own and her mother's, to add richness to the images presented and to fix the photographs in a particular time and place.

The poem opens 10 years *"before"* Duffy was born, just at the end of the Second World War, when the photograph was taken. She is standing on a street corner, arms linked with her best friends, Maggie and Jean. Duffy's uses *colloquial language*[28]to give authenticity to the memory – *"pals"*, as young people today would say *"mates"*, instead of the more formal *"friends"*. Their carefree happiness is conveyed by the *"bend from the waist"*

---

[28] *Colloquial language* is the language that people speak, as opposed to a more formal written language.

and "*shriek*" as they are doubled up with laughter. "*Marilyn*" is a reference to Marilyn Monroe in the famous scene from "*The Seven Year Itch*" (1955) where she stands over a subway vent in New York and her dress blows up around her. This is anachronistic[29] as her mother would not have known the film at this time – it is Duffy using an image familiar to her, to describe how her mother appeared to her in the photograph.

The opening statement of the second stanza, "*I'm not here yet*", confirms that the poem recalls a time before Duffy was born. She refers to another photograph taken at a dance. Her mother has no idea that she will bear a daughter, as she dances in the "*ballroom*", where dances, both ballroom dancing and "jive" or "rock and roll", would have been held at this time. In the 60s, they became "discos" and are now "clubs". The "*thousand eyes*" is a reference to the song *The Night has a Thousand Eyes* (1962) first made popular by Bobby Vee, a pop star of the 60s. Again, Duffy is using references from her own youth to describe her mother's experience, perhaps so that she can relate to her mother's experiences more directly and show the similarities between them. Her mother is hoping to meet a boy; the "*fizzy, movie tomorrows*" are the hope for a date after the cinema, if the "*right*" boy walks her home. "*I knew you would dance like that*" shows that, before, Duffy has imagined her mother when she was young – now she has actual proof of those imaginings in the photographs. Her Mother is going to be late home from the dance; her mother, "*Ma*", Duffy's grandmother, will be waiting at the corner of the road where she lives and she will be punished for it. "*Hiding*" means a "*spanking*" although that is probably an exaggeration. Anyway, the young girl doesn't care – she has had fun. Again, "*Ma*" and "*hiding*" are *colloquial* terms, recalling the speech of the place and time.

---

[29] *Anachronistic* means wrong for the time period. A notable example is a film where Julius Caesar was shown wearing a watch.

In stanza three, the Mother's past and the child's begin to merge after she is born, and is about six years old. In the opening line, Duffy suggests that she knows that her mother's life was happiest, and she was most free to enjoy herself, in the ten years of her late adolescence and early adulthood, before she was married and had Duffy, who demanded her attention with her *"possessive yell"*. Once married and with a child, her mother's life would have been restricted to the home and domestic duties; it was not the "done thing" for mothers to go out by themselves or with friends to dances. The *colloquial* *"eh?"* addresses the line directly to her mother. She remembers pretending to "walk" in her mother's high heeled shoes, putting her hands inside them. They are *"relics"*, sacred objects, from her mother's youth which leads to the idea of her being a "ghost" from the past. This memory conjures up a vivid picture of her mother wearing those high-heeled shoes, that *"clatter"* as she walks, until it is as if she is standing right next to Duffy, who can smell her perfume and see the love bites on her neck. The line is framed as a question to her mother: *"who gave you the love bites?"* and the term *"sweetheart"* borrowed from the speech of the boy that gave them to her.

The final stanza recalls a time when they were together, the mother's dancing days long gone, but she still recalls the steps of the dances of her youth, and teaches them to her daughter: *"Cha cha cha!* The contrast between her life now and then is made by the *"coming home from Mass"*; she is being a good, dutiful Catholic, all thoughts of dancing and fun behind her. But even so, she stamps out *"stars"* – as Duffy says, little sparks from the nails in the mended heels of her shoes. The "wrong pavement" refers back to the first stanza; that was in Glasgow, this is in Stafford. There is poignancy and affection in this juxtaposition of the former and present life; it has gone, but it is not forgotten, and she wants to pass some of its joy on to the child. Duffy regretted *"even then"* that she did not know this young version of her mother. What she admires is her boldness and carefree youthfulness, the touch of glamour that she brings to her life, conveyed by the word *"sparkle"* and the repeated *"ands"*[30] to pick out each feature of her mother and bring her vividly to life. The poem comes full circle with the last words *"before you were mine"*, joining the ideas about what her mother has lost, how grateful her daughter is for the sacrifice, and the love between them.

---

[30] This form of repetition, when you repeat conjunction, is called *polysyndeton*: *"sparkle **and** waltz **and** laugh"*

Winter Swans – Owen Sheers

Context

The Welsh poet, novelist and dramatist Owen Sheers is the youngest writer in the collection. He is perhaps best known for his verse-drama *"Pink Mist"* (2013), based on the stories of three young soldiers deployed to Afghanistan and their return home to those left behind, which was dramatized by the BBC. The BBC also commissioned *"A Poet's Guide to Britain"* (2009), an anthology of poems chosen by Sheers, evoking the spirit of Place, which was accompanied by a documentary. This poem comes from his second collection, *"Skirrid Hill"* (2005).

Sheers's poetry is often described as *"lyrical"* and *"musical"*. He writes about separation, loss and the relationship between people and landscape.

Themes

This is another poem about **relationships between men and women.** This poem, Elizabeth Barrett's *"Sonnet"*, Dooley's *"Letters…"* and Nagra's *"Singh Song!"* are the most **positive representations of relationships between men and women** in the cluster. Like many other poems in the anthology, the poem evokes the landscape and the weather, placing the poet and his subject within it, making them part of a universal whole. In this, he is reminiscent of Heaney. Like Shelley in *"Love's Philosophy"*, the poet takes a lesson from nature. Shelley looks at the natural landscape for a model of how men and women should come together; Sheers looks at the Swans as an example of the possibility, and desirability, of a lasting, loving relationship. Sheers' poem is initially tinged with a feeling of separation; the lovers seem to be *"apart"*, emotionally and physically, at the beginning. However, by the end the Swans have taught them to *"swim"* the distance created between them and re-unite.

Form, Structure and Language

The poem is in *free verse*, each line made up of predominantly three or four stressed syllables, which give it a measured tread, as of them slowly walking. This three- and four-beat rhythm is extended to five beats at lines 9 and 11, to reflect the image of the swans dipping their heads and necks into the water, and then rising back to the surface.

The poem opens after *"two days of rain"*, with the lovers taking the opportunity of a break in the weather to go for a walk together. The positioning of the word *"break"* at the end of the second line, although referring to the weather, foreshadows the suggestion in line 6 that the two have had a disagreement, as they walk *"silent and apart."* This suggestion is also present in the *personification* of the saturated earth *"gulping for breath"*, and the verb *"skirted"*, which means to edge around, as if they are avoiding intimacy.

The action of the swans *"stops"* them; they both stop walking and also pause in their quarrel, united in watching. The third and fourth stanzas contain images of separation and coming together, in the *"tipping in unison"*; the *"halved themselves"*; *"icebergs"*, which float alone, and in *"boats righting"*, weathering the storm. The *"rough weather"* is a *metaphor* for their disagreement.

In the fifth stanza, the partner links the swans and the couple in the reference to the swans' mating habits, perhaps wistfully, perhaps innocently. Whichever, the effect is to draw them together again. *"Porcelain"* is a delicate, white china; the suggestion of fragility is recognition of the possibility of relationships breaking. The water *"stills"* as the birds move away, again a reference to their previous quarrel. The "troubled waters" of their disagreement have now quietened down.

In the sixth stanza, the two continue walking, but the poet realises that, unconsciously, and as if in response to the example of the mated swans, they are now holding hands. Notice that they are now no longer *"skirting"* the lake, but *"slow-stepping"* together at the lakes edge in the *"shingle and sand"*, almost entering the swans' watery environment. Their hands have metaphorically "swum" across the *"distance between"* them.

The final couplet completes the image of unity, with the hands folded together like the closed wings of a swan *"after flight"*, a reminder of their former separation.

Singh Song! – Daljit Nagra

Context

Daljit Nagra is a poet who sometimes uses the distinctive dialect of Indians whose first language is Punjabi (sometimes called *"Punglish"*) to affectionately characterise their experience of living in Britain, often with comic effect. He is himself a first-generation, English-born Sikh whose parents came to Britain in the late 1950s and owned a shop. The poem is included in his debut collection of poems *"Look Who is Coming to Dover!"*, which won the 2007 Forward prize for Poetry.

The setting of the poem is a corner shop owned by the speaker's father. Throughout the mid- to late-20th century, Indian immigrants brought up corner shops across Britain, working long hours to supply a local, and growing, market for convenience foods, possibly as a result of more women going to work and having less time for regular grocery shopping. These shops are slowly being supplanted by the local branches of the large supermarkets, such as Tesco Local, and being sold by their owners because their children now go to university and aspire to professional careers.

Nagra has described his poetry as "taking the lid off" the lives of immigrant families in Britain. You can find a video of him talking about this poem here:
http://poetrystation.org.uk/poems/daljit-nagra-talks-about-singh-song and here:
https://www.youtube.com/watch?v=nYIDS4Ka7CE

Themes

This is a comic love poem; a *dramatic monologue* written in praise of the wife of a young man who keeps one of his father's chain of corner shops. Like *"Winter Swans"*, *"Sonnet"* and *"Letters..."*, this is a poem which presents **a positive view of relationships between men and women.** In its explicit references to female sexuality, it reflects modern attitudes and can be contrasted with the poems of Byron and Shelley, where the focus is on male desire. It also explores **the generation and culture gap** between Singh and his wife, and his family. The poem explores his love in the context of Singh's parents' culture and the culture within which he and his wife live, dispelling the idea that the Indian or Sikh culture is homogenous; this next generation of young people has grown up in a very different culture, reflected in their speech and attitudes. The generation gap is also explored in Waterhouse's *"Climbing My Grandfather"*, in a very different context, and in Duffy's *"Before You Were Mine"*.

The title is a pun on the expression "sing-song" meaning having the rhythm and rhyme of a song. *"Singh"* is Nagra's middle name and he has adopted it as the name of his *persona*, the young man who minds the shop. The poem is structured, like a pop song, ABC/ABC/AD. Section A provides the narrative, setting the scenes, and is written in a regular four-beat rhythm; section B focuses on Singh and his bride and their lovemaking, written in a sing-song *disyllabic* rhythm; section C gives us the *chorus* of shoppers, again in four-beat rhythm. The final section D is a "love-duet" between Singh and his bride, as in a Bollywood movie. There is also a variable, but noticeable, use of rhyme which adds to the "sing-song" effect.

The whole is written in *"Punglish"* (which is not Nagra's dialect, as he speaks and writes in standard English), a dialect reflecting the pronunciation, grammar and vocabulary of people whose first language is Punjabi and who have acquired English as an additional language.

The first stanza (Section A) establishes the central comic setting: downstairs is the shop where the young man works for his father; upstairs is where he and his "bride" live and make love. Instead of minding the shop, Singh uses the quiet moments between customers to lock up the shop and sneak up stairs. The difference in expectations between the generations, father and son, is shown in the *"he vunt me not to hav a break"*.

Stanza two (Section B) introduces the bride, as the two of them make love and snack together. The comic intent of the poem, and its contrasting of the two cultures, is evident in the joke *"rowing through Putney"*, a reference to the Oxford-Cambridge boat race from Putney to Mortlake, an iconic event in the British sporting calendar.

Singh's absence from the shop (Section C – stanza 3) is heralded by a chorus of shoppers expressing their disapproval of him and his neglected shop. There is also a suggestion that these are white British shoppers, complaining at the unfamiliarity of the goods on offer: *"lemons/limes"*, *"bananas/plaintains"*.

The generation gap is shown in the fourth stanza (Section A repeat), where his thoroughly modern Indian wife is surfing the net on her computer and playing with men on a Sikh dating site, like a *"cat"* plays with a *"mouse"*, baiting them with *"meat"* and *"cheese"* – another punning use, this time of the word *"mouse"*.

This thought of his bride leads Singh to *eulogise* (praise) her in a *refrain*. (Section B repeat – stanzas 5 - 7). She does not show the kind of respect for Singh's parents normally expected in the stereotype of a Sikh girl; she swears at Singh's mother in Punjabi and imitates his father. Nor is she conventionally beautiful, with her small, sharp eyes and round stomach. She doesn't dress like one either, with her dyed, short red hair, her sari in the pattern of Scots national dress, and her flat shoes in which she can chase shoplifters. However, his affection for her, and his admiration of her independence, is evident in the repeated *"my bride"* and the *alliterated "tummy of a teddy"*.

The *chorus* of shoppers returns (Section C – stanza 8) to complain of his absence again, this time that his goods are stale and old, making it the *"worst"* shop in the road.

In stanza 9, the narrative returns, to tell what happens after the shop has closed (Section A repeat). *"in di midnight hour"* is a reference to the famous pop-song by Wilson Pickett *"In the Midnight Hour"* (1966): *"I'm gonna wait 'til the midnight hour/when there's no-one else around."* Nagra uses a variety of sensual images in this stanza. The street is described with the *alliterative "concrete-cool"* after the heat of the day. *"whispering stairs"*, is *hypallage*, or a *transferred epithet*[31] as it is the lovers who *"whisper"*, not the stairs that they come down. The metal stool is *"silver"*, also suggesting the reflection of the *"brightey moon"*, which shines down, past the crowded shop windows, on an imaginary *"beach"*.

Against this Bollywood backdrop, the two lovers begin their love-duet (Section D), each sitting on a stool. Each line begins with the same words, *"from di stool each night..."*, showing that they are in harmony with each other. She asks him for the price of the moon; he replies that it is worth half of what she is worth, and, in response to her questioning how much that is, he replies that she is *"priceless"*. In contrast to the comedy that has gone before, these final lines have an innocent playfulness and sincerity in the echoed *"baby"* by which they address each other, which affirm their love for one another.

---

[31] *hypallage*, or a *transferred epithet,* is to switch the subject and object of an adjective or verb.

Climbing My Grandfather – Andrew Waterhouse

Context

In 2000, Waterhouse won the Forward Prize for Best First Collection, one of the most prestigious awards for Poetry in Britain, for his collection *"in"*. It seems that few were aware of the depression that led to his suicide less than two years later. Waterhouse's poetry is rooted in landscape and the natural world. Just before he died, he bought 10 acres of Northumbrian hillside on which he planted a new wood of forty trees. This poem reflects this engagement with landscape, in the detailing of the mountain which forms the basis of the *extended metaphor*[32] of the child's "climb".

Themes

Uniquely in the cluster, this poem explores **the relationship between a child and a grandparent.** The greater **generational gap** is perhaps reflected in the way the poet focuses on the physical characteristics of the old man, rather than his personality, and his lack of interaction with the child. The child has no memory of the life of the older man; he only has testimony to how the grandfather has lived his life in the physical marks on his body. So, the child explores his grandfather and their relationship to each other not through his memory of a shared activity (as Heaney does in *"Follower"* or Armitage in *"Mother…"*) nor through images of his past life (as Duffy does in *"Before You Were Mine"* or Causley in *"Eden Rock"*) but in his physicality and the contrast between the solidity of his form and the agility of the climbing child. The poem is an *extended metaphor;* the child climbs up the grandfather as if climbing a mountain. The poem uses the

---

[32] An *extended metaphor* is a metaphor with many points of comparison between the two things being compared.

semantic field of mountain-climbing and exaggerates the size of the components of the man's body and clothes to sustain the metaphor, magnifying the difference in size between the child and the adult. This gives to the old man a stature and grandeur which reflects the child's feelings for him and also suggests the generational gap between them; although he is familiar and accessible physically, the old man remains largely unknown both emotionally and psychologically.

The poem is written in one long stanza with lines which have predominantly four stresses, becoming five as the *"summit"* of the grandfather's head is reached and he rests. This suggests the upward momentum of the child, climbing without pause.

The poem opens with the child's decision to *"do it free"*, meaning to make the climb without harness or safety equipment, which makes it more dangerous. This suggests that the child does not know what dangers lie ahead, nor what he will discover on his "climb", and also that he is testing himself; this is unfamiliar territory.

He starts at the feet, the *"old brogues"* at once epitomising the generational gap between them. *"Brogues"* are leather shoes which are now old-fashioned, or worn by men in stolid professions, probably handmade when his grandfather bought them and frequently mended. They are *"dusty and cracked"*, suggesting that they have been well worn and that the old man no longer needs to keep them polished and serviceable, as his working and walking days are behind him.

Climbing up his legs is easy, the word *"scramble"* suggests both the child's size and his initial eagerness at these lower levels, as he can grab on to the thick material, like finding a multitude of fissures in a rock face in which to put his feet and hands in his "climb".

Just below the waistband, where the old man's shirt overhangs his trousers, the child changes direction, to go sideways. Note the use of *enjambment* on *"change/direction"*, rather like Heaney's use to show the changing direction of the plough in *"Follower"*. He uses the belt as a ledge to cross over to the old man's hand.

Waterhouse uses the *enjambment* of *"nails/are splintered"*, this time to capture the detail of the hand. The *"splintered"* nails and the hand being *"earth-stained"* suggest a life spent working on the land; Waterhouse himself was brought up in an urban environment in Lincolnshire, which may again suggest a generational gap. Waterhouse uses an *oxymoron*[33], *"warm ice"*, to describe the feel of his skin; it is smooth but, unlike ice, transmits a warmth from the heat of his blood, an idea which recurs at the end of the poem. The idea of smoothness is continued with the likening of the scar on his arm to a *"glassy ridge"*, as if the boy is now climbing a potentially treacherous glacier. Maybe the child wonders how this scar was made but is reluctant to open old wounds – hence him placing his feet *"gently in the old stitches"*. The old man had a life which is hidden from the child, who can only explore its outer manifestations, and some of those manifestations hint at danger.

This idea of hidden danger (of memories?) lying beneath the physical presence of the old man is again hinted at in the child *"not looking down"* from his safe vantage point at the man's *"firm shoulder"*. For the moment, he is safe, resting comfortably, but *"climbing has its dangers"*; exploring this man can bring the unexpected. *"Looking down"* is also *"looking back"* and, given the poet's birthdate (and one can assume this poem is autobiographical), it might not be too fanciful to think

---

[33] An *oxymoron* is a juxtaposition of words with opposite meanings, as in *bitter sweet*.

that the underlying danger may lie in stirring up memories of the First World War, in which his grandfather may have received the scar. Men of his generation rarely spoke about their experiences in the war, even to close family. The child senses, and the adult poet perhaps knows, of his grandfather's inner life.

After a brief pause, the child moves on, having to *"pull"* himself up the increasingly loose terrain of his *"neck"* and *"cheek"*. His mouth is like a spring, from which he can drink, before he heads across the uneven terrain of his *"cheek"* and up to his eye. In the *"slowly open and close"* the poet conveys the monumental solidity of the figure of the old man, as if he were some kind of mountain giant that the child has discovered.

With a final push, conveyed by the *enjambment* of *"up over/the forehead"*, the child, using the *"wrinkles"* of the man's forehead as a ladder, approaches the summit, the top of the old man's head. The man's hair is *"white"*, *"soft"* and *"thick"* like snow on the summit of his head. Having reached his goal, the child rests, exhausted.

In the child watching the *"clouds and birds circle"* there is a feeling of both achievement and freedom, of having reached a higher plane where the world lies mapped out below him. However, he is still firmly connected to that world through the warm pulsing of the old man's heart. Compare this with Armitage's image of his mother holding the very edge of the tape-measure as her son contemplates whether he will *"fall or fly"*. The simple adjective *"good"* conveys the affection the child and the adult poet feel for this old man; it is a judgement on the way the man has lived his life; on the quality of the relationship between them; on the solidity of his physical presence and the hope that the heart will continue to beat.

Power and Conflict

Introduction to the Romantic Poets

There is one thing that *any fule kno*[34] about the "Big Five" Romantic poets – they died in reverse order to being born. So, Wordsworth (1770 – 1850), Coleridge (1772 – 1834), Byron (1788-1824) Shelley (1792 – 1822), Keats (1795 – 1821). To this group may be added William Blake (1757 – 1827), although his poetry is distinctive. Blake is discussed in the introduction to the poem "*London*".

The Romantic movement, or *Romanticism*, was a reaction to the preceding Age of Enlightenment, which valued rational, scientific thought above the revelation of emotions, the imagination, and the transforming power of the natural world. Wordsworth, in his preface to "*The Lyrical Ballads*" (1798), which he co-authored with Coleridge, described poetry as the "*spontaneous overflow of powerful feelings*". Romantic Poetry is characterised by a *focus on the sensibilities:* a recognition of the "*sublime*" in the natural world; a willingness to engage in the imaginative possibilities of a supernatural world which co-exists with ours; the expression of intense emotions; a questioning of the nature of Art and aesthetics and the creative process; an exploration of spirituality, religious beliefs and the meaning of life. *Medievalism* and *Gothic* are sub-genres of *Romanticism*. *Medievalism* harks back to the legends of King Arthur and the Knights of the Round Table, and the conventions of chivalry and courtly love, with idealised relationships between men and women. *Medievalism* provides the setting for the *Gothic*, but in *Gothic* the focus is on the supernatural, and the relationships between men and women are often highly eroticised. The poets were also revolutionary in their support for the overthrow of the established order through non-violent protest and championed the plight of the working poor.

---

[34] Molesworth in "*Down with Skool*" (sic), G. Willans. 1953.

The poets were anxious to break away from the rigid rules of poesy, such as the strict use of rhythm and rhyme, exhibited by earlier poets such as Alexander Pope (1688 – 1744), seeking for a more natural rhythm, closer to speech, and a more colloquial *lexis*.[35] Wordsworth, in the introduction to *"Lyrical Ballads"* (1802) declared his intention to write in *"the language really spoken by men"*. However, many of their earlier poems are written in prescribed forms – such as *sonnets* – and their poems often do have a regular rhythm and a regular rhyme scheme.

---

[35] *Lexis* is vocabulary

Ozymandias – Percy Bysshe Shelley

Context

If the name "Shelley" is familiar, but not the poet, this is because it was his second wife, Mary Wollstonecraft Shelley, who wrote the Gothic novel *"Frankenstein"*, whilst on holiday in Geneva with Shelley, Byron and John Polidori, who wrote the early vampire novel, *"The Vampyre"*. Shelley and his circle were unconventional, if not scandalous, for their time but were well-connected and wealthy and could largely afford to ignore public and private criticism, although they were at times estranged from their families. They believed in the supremacy of the individual spirit over convention and rules, indulging in multiple relationships and declaring their atheism.

"Ozymandias" was written in 1817/18, possibly inspired by the disinterment of the statue of the Egyptian God-King Rameses II in Thebes, which was acquired by the British Museum. *"Ozymandias"* is the Greek form of the name of the Pharaoh.

Themes

The poem shows **the mortality of Man and his works** against a **greater power,** in this case **Time.** Man's *hubris* (pride) in the face of **Time** is a theme also explored by Imtiaz Dharker in *"Tissue"*. Wordsworth also shows man confronted by a power which is beyond his understanding in the extract from *"The Prelude"*, in this case **the power of nature**, as does Heaney in *"Storm on the Island"*. In the depiction of a ruler who is **contemptuous of those he rules**, *Ozymandias* has similarities with the Duke in *"My Last Duchess"*. Like Wordsworth, Shelley is also showing **the power of imagination** to conjure up deep feelings from the world he observes.

Form, Structure and Language

The poem is "a tale within a tale", as the narrative voice of the poet – the "I" of the opening line – gives way to that of the *traveller*, who recounts what he has seen in the desert. This removes Shelley from directly commenting on the statue, or its implications. The ironic "message" - that however powerful a man may be in life, he will become powerless in the face of Time - lies in Shelley's juxtaposition of the lyrical description of the statue with the "quote" from the base of the ruined monument.

The poem is in *sonnet* form; there are fourteen lines of predominantly *iambic pentametre*[36] with a fairly regular rhyme scheme. This formal structure is in keeping with the subject matter – solid blocks of masonry lying in the desert which have been unearthed, perhaps by sandstorms and erosion. Notice that Heaney's poem is also written in regular *iambic pentametre*, giving it the same solidity, like the squat houses built into the rock and roofed with slate to stand against the storm. Both Wordsworth and Heaney, however, write in *blank verse* – unrhyming lines.

Shelley makes considerable use of *enjambment* and *caesura* to bring his imagined scene to life and animate the long-dead face of the king. Shelley first uses *enjambment* to place the parts of his ruined statue in this desert scene, with the line *"legs of stone/Stand"*, reversing the usual *iambic* beat (ti-**TUM**) and using a *dactyl* (**TUM**-ti-ti) to put emphasis on *"Stand"*:

> Two **vast**/ and **trunk**/less **legs**/ of **stone**/
> **Stand** in the/**des**ert./

---

[36] *Iambic pentametre* is five metric *feet* in a line, each *foot* having a pattern of light - heavy beats (ti-**TUM**). See the section on *"Metre"* at the end of this Guide.

He follows this up in lines 3 and 4 with the run-on from *"sand"* to *"Half-sunk"*, which "sinks" the *"visage"* in the middle of the line:

Near them/ **on** the/ **sand**/
Half sunk, / a **shat**/tered **vis**/age **lies**, ...

He also uses an *internal rhyme*[37] *"stand/sand"* to tie the beginning and end of the line together, keeping the structure tight. Notice also how Shelley has arranged the syntax to start line 6 with the command word *"Tell"*; this is what the traveller is doing, telling us a tale, but it also introduces the idea of the ancient King's power and authority.

Focus now moves to the king's face, which in spite of being *"shattered"*, retains the signs of his previous authority. *"Frown/wrinkled lip/sneer"* all suggest the contempt he has for those beneath him. Shelley uses the alliterated consonant *"c"* in *"cold command"* and later *"sculptor"* to convey the harshness of the king's regime. The sculptor has captured the king's emotions well – he has *"stamped"* them into the stones for eternity. There is some ambiguity in line 8. This is more likely to be referring to the king than the sculptor; *"the hand"* being the king's, mocking both his subjects and the *"Mighty"* who are addressed on the pedestal, and the heart being *"fed"* by their supplication. This is a rhetorical device call *synecdoche*, where a part of something (*"hand/heart"*) is used in place of the whole thing (*"king"*).

Line 8 also marks the *volta* or "turn" in the direction of the poem; the rhyme scheme momentarily becomes uneven at this point as if to indicate the switch. The first eight lines (the *octet*) have described the broken statue and the aspect of the king.

---

[37] *Internal rhyme* is a rhyme within a line, rather than at the end.

The eighth line turns our attention to the pedestal beneath. The following six lines (the *sestet)* quote the engraving. Lines 10 and 11 are a command from the long-dead King to his subjects and his conquered enemies, to *"despair!"*. How can they ever hope to reach the heights of power and majesty that he, Ozymandias, has? They are beaten even before they attempt to overthrow him. Statues to Egyptian King-Gods demonstrated, through their sheer size, their immense power and invulnerability.

However, the message of the traveller is ironic. Ozymandias may have felt invulnerable in the face of his enemies, but **Time** can, and will, overcome even the mightiest of Kings. Ozymandias's *"works"* have crumbled to dust and the broken statue is all that remains of his power. Shelley splits line 12 into two, using the *caesura* to make his bald statement of futility: *"Nothing beside remains."* He then runs the end of the line onto the next to emphasise *"colossal wreck"*, a juxtaposition of images which creates *bathos* – an anti-climax under-pinning his theme.

In the last two lines Shelley conveys the vast nothingness which surrounds these relics by extensive use of *alliteration* and open vowel sounds: *"boundless and bare"*; the repeated "l" sounds in *"lone/level"*; the alliterated *"sands stretch"*. He also plays with inverting the *iambic* metre at *"boundless"*, using a *trochee,* and at *"stretch far",* using a *spondee,* to slow the lines, opening up the vastness of the surrounding desert.

London – William Blake

Context

Like other Romantics, Blake challenges the supremacy of rational, scientific thought, seeking for spirituality and the transforming power of the imagination in human lives. He was a visionary and mystic, as well as a painter and engraver. Much of his poetry is the poetry of *"radical protest"*[38], championing the plight of the urban poor. Prior to the "Industrial Revolution", Britain was largely an agrarian economy – one based on the production of materials from the countryside, primarily food and wool. "The Industrial Revolution" is the name given to the period between, roughly, the mid-18th century and the middle of the 19th century which shifted Britain from an economy based on agriculture to one based on manufacturing. It was made possible by a series of inventions and developments in, particularly, textiles, steam power and iron making. Taken together, these inventions and developments in engineering replaced the cottage industries and led to a move of the majority of the population away from the countryside into the towns where the new factories were often sited. By 1851, half the population of Britain lived in towns. This shift led to considerable social challenges, including pressure on housing, sanitation and water provision. It also required changes to traditional working patterns which, in a rural environment (largely determined by the cycle of day and night and the seasons) had been the norm, but, in an industrial setting, imposed terrible hardships on men, women and children – long hours without respite, seven days a week working and children working in mines and factories at a very young age.

---

[38] Peter Ackroyd at http://www.bbc.co.uk/arts/romantics/intro.shtml

Blake was born and lived in London all his life. The poem "London" is taken from the collection "Songs of Experience" (1794), a counterpart to "Songs of Innocence" (1789), which Blake describes on the cover of the combined volume as "the two contrary states of the human soul". Childhood, for the Romantics, was a time of innocence, in that it was unconstrained by the conventions of society and the stifling authority of Church and State. "Experience" is the exposure to these corrupting influences, against which Blake protests. This poem is a condemnation of a ruling class that ignores the plight of the urban poor and is blind to the hardships caused by the Government's failure to respond to societal change.

Themes

In the focus on the **conflict between Man and Society**, Blake's poem has links with Agard's "Checking Out Me History" (which also uses the rhythm and rhymes of songs) and Garland's "Kamikaze". The subjects of each of these poems are to an extent trapped within the conventions of a society which does not recognise their individuality or autonomy. Agard rails against the revisionist history of the British Empire, which excludes the stories of black protagonists, whilst "Kamikaze" shows how society ostracizes a man who follows his conscience rather than convention. Both Shelley and Blake were considered "dangerous" in their expression of ideas that challenged conventional norms.

Form, Structure and Language

In keeping with the title, many of Blake's poems are written in simple, song-like rhythms with much repetition. The *metre* is regular *iambic tetrametre* (four stresses in a line of *iambs* – ti-TUM) and has a regular *abab* rhyme scheme. Much of the poem's effectiveness lies in the contrast between this sing-song form and the serious subject matter, the repetition hammering home the message of lives robbed of the uplifting power of imagination and spirit, because they are impoverished by the oppression of the State, Commerce and the Church.

The opening stanza places the poet in the streets of London, the word *"wander"* suggesting familiarity with his surroundings and also the universality of the sights and sounds around him – he does not have to search them out. *"Chartered"* means here *"managed for profit"*, as a *"charter"* was a licence to trade. Not only are the streets he walks through bound to the *"profit motive"*, but even the natural flow of the River Thames has become bound and confined by the same motive; the Thames was a major shipping route, bringing goods and raw materials, particularly coal, from the Pool of London in the east, and was bounded by wharves and warehouses on both banks.

As he *"wanders"*, Blake notes the faces of the people he passes, which seem to bear signs of frailty and sorrow. Note how Blake changes the regular *iambic* rhythm here to emphasise the word *"Marks"*. He *inverts* (turns around) the ti-**Tum** of the *iamb* to create a *trochee* (**Tum**-ti):

*"**Marks** of /**weak**ness/, **marks** of/ **woe**"*

This line is called a *trochaic tetrametre* – three full feet of *trochees* plus one incomplete foot – which is called *catalexis*[39]. This is the rhythm of Blake's most famous poem *"The Tyger"*:

*__Tyg__er/, __tyg__er,/ __burn__ing/ __bright__
__In__ the __for__ests __of__ the __night__*

Stanza 2, with the repeated *"every"* continues the idea of ubiquity – no-one in this city is free from the blight. *"Every man"* is probably also to be read as "Everyman", the

_____

[39] A *catalectic* line is one that has an incomplete *metric foot* at the end.

eponymous hero of the medieval morality play that follows the journey of an ordinary man through his life. The stanza depicts the sounds of woe as the people cry out in their pain. *"Every ban"* is most likely to be a reference to the notices read out in church before a marriage, as in *"reading the ban(n)s"*, which would reflect Blake's own views on the institution of marriage, and foreshadows the last lines of the poem. They are bound to a life which imprisons them, both body and soul. The *"mind-forged manacles"* are a *metaphor* for the suppression of the imagination and spirit of people who are trapped in this corrupt society and its conventions.

Stanza 3 moves from the general to the specific – giving examples of the cries of the *"Every man"* of the previous stanza. First, the cry of the child chimney-sweep is heard. Fires in London were fuelled by coal, which leaves a dense black soot, requiring regular brushing to avoid chimney fires. Small boys were sent up the chimneys to sweep them out, a dangerous, at times fatal, occupation. Their plight was made famous in the book *"The Water Babies"* (1863) by Charles Kingsley, which Blake anticipated by some years. The *"black'ning church"* is a comment on the attitude of the church towards this horror – it is *"black'ning"*, as all buildings in London did, from the soot deposits, and should be protesting against the toll taken on the sweeps. The next image is of a soldier dying for his country. The soldier is *"hapless"* as he has no choice whether to fight or not. His *"sigh"* is both a cry of helplessness and his dying breath. This is an example of how Blake moves from the literal (a sighing soldier) to the visionary – the sigh becomes an image of blood on the walls. In this stanza, Blake is making an ironic comment on a society which allows this to happen. Both institutions – Church and Crown/State are complicit in the pain of the oppressed.

In Stanza 4, Blake reserves his harshest criticism for the institution of marriage. Blake believed in a God, or supreme being, but was deeply critical of the Church as an organisation, seeing it as an instrument for the suppression of individual liberty and freedom of thought. He saw the institution of marriage as a shackling of man's nature and instincts, particularly in the elevation of Chastity and Marriage as virtues in themselves, regardless of how men and women felt about their relationships with one another. As he wanders through the streets at night, he hears the cries of the young prostitutes, of whom there were many thousands in London, although it is not clear that all were what we would call "prostitutes" today. This term was also applied to unmarried women living with men, or unmarried mothers. The plight of unmarried mothers was particularly harsh, and Blake imagines how their instinct to soothe their child when it cries is transformed into a *"curse"* as they regret having given birth. He then expands this vision to show how the fate of these poor unfortunates is bound up with the lives of the "respectable marrieds". Instead of a "carriage", the newly-weds travel in a *"hearse"* – a vehicle for carrying coffins. This is a comment on, first, the deadening institution of marriage, which at the time, was often arranged or subject to strict societal conventions, which might not reflect the desires of the couple. Second, and more sinisterly, *"plagues"* is a reference to sexually transmitted infections, commonly gonorrhoea or the deadly syphilis, transmitted by these "prostitutes". Unmarried men visited prostitutes because respectable unmarried women were expected to remain "chaste" until marriage. The men contracted a STI which they then passed to their wives, which, with few effective treatments, resulted in infertility in the woman, or death.

This is a bleak, apocalyptic view of society, of which London is seen as the pinnacle of all that is wrong.

Extract from *"The Prelude"* – William Wordsworth

Context

Described by Wordsworth as *"the poem on the growth of my own mind"*, *"The Prelude"* was intended to precede *"The Recluse"*, which he never finished. Essentially, it charts, over 14 books, the influence of Nature and the French Revolution, on his sensibilities as a poet. The extract selected here, taken from *Book 1 - Boyhood* could be described as one of the *"spots in time"* that Wordsworth identified as formative moments in his understanding of himself and the world around him:

There are in our existence spots of time,
That with distinct pre-eminence retain
A renovating virtue,   *Prelude Book*
XII

The Romantics took themselves seriously as men who, through their poetry, could help others understand the world around them. The creative process and the workings of the imagination were worth exploration in themselves, giving us an insight into our relationship to both our place in the physical world around us (loosely defined as "Nature") and how we might tap into powers beyond the merely physical. In another age, this could be equated with "religion", but the Romantics were, primarily, atheists and did not equate this awareness of spirituality with any established religion.

Themes

The poem reflects on **the power of nature**, of the **imagination** and of **memory**. Sometimes referred to as *"The Stolen Boat"*, the extract describes the young Wordsworth's night-time escapade in a boat. He sets out to row across Ullswater Lake in the Lake District, where he lived for much of his life. Fixing his eyes on the top of a hill to keep his line straight as he rows, as he gets further and further away from this point, slowly a much taller peak emerges from behind it. This causes him to be filled with a kind of guilty dread, so he heads back home. The older poet uses this *"spot in time"* to reflect on the power of **"unknown modes of being"** – things which we cannot know through our five senses and which we strive to understand spiritually or imaginatively. The crag rising in front of him is both physically powerful and stirs imaginings which bring with them feelings of guilt, dread and helplessness in the face of an unknown real or imagined power.

The poem can be linked thematically to Shelley's *"Ozymandias"* in reflecting on **the power of nature** or of powers beyond man's control. It also explores the **power of memory** to haunt the imagination, as does Armitage in *"Remains"*, where the image of the dead enemy returns to haunt his dreams, and Weir in *"Poppies"*, where she recalls memories of her son's childhood.

Form, Structure and Language

The extract starts as a *narrative*[40] written in *blank verse:* unrhymed lines of *iambic pentametre.* The reader is guided to the meaning by the use of *enjambment* and *caesura,* placing stresses on important words and allowing variation in the rhythm and pace. As often in Wordsworth, the narrative of the opening lines (to line 20) gives way to increased *lyricism*[41] and a change of mood or viewpoint (lines 21 – 34) and ends in reflection or contemplation (line 35 to end).

The extract opens conversationally enough, although the *"(led by her)"* tells us a little about Wordsworth and his intense

---

[40] *Narrative* is a story.
[41] *Lyrical* poetry is poetry that tells of deep feelings or thoughts.

relationship to the natural world, as he *personifies*[42] nature as "*her*". His unties the boat and gets in seemingly without hesitation. Note the positioning of "*Straight*" at the beginning of line 4, varying the *iambic* rhythm to emphasise the word, and the similar weighting of "*Pushed*" in line 5, by the use of the *enjambment* from the preceding line, giving these lines a forward momentum to mimic the movement of the boat.

"Straight I un/**loosed** her/ **chain**, and/ **stepping**/ **in**
Pushed from the /**shore**...

He admits to feeling a little guilty about his activity and suggests that nature ("*Mountain-echoes*") has something to say about it. However, he gives himself up to the pleasures of the moment on his boat ride, indicated by the light imagery of "*glittering*", "*melted*", "*sparkling*". His positive attitude continues with the description of the night sky; the use of the word "*elfin*" suggests that this night is enchanted and special.

The dream begins to turn into a nightmare at line 21, when, behind the crag on which he has "*fixed [his] view*", a higher peak begins to loom up in the darkness. This peak at once appears threatening, as shown by the use of *repetition:* "*a huge peak, black and huge*". It too is *personified*, this time as a monster which "*upreared its head*". The leisurely rowing gives way to an almost frantic attempt to get away from its presence, in the repeated "*struck and struck again*", but the "*grim shape*" seems to be following him like a malevolent giant. The words here show its intent: "*Towered*", "*purpose*", "*measured*", "*Strode*". Note the positioning of the words "*Towered*", following the *enjambment*, and "*Strode*" at the beginning of the lines for emphasis. The only way to "escape" this monster is, paradoxically, to turn around and row back to land, back

---

[42] *Personification* is attributing human characteristics to non-human things

towards it (line 29). Now the mood is very different: "*trembling*", "*silent*", "*stole*", "*covert*[43]", "*grave*", "*serious*". No time now for watching moonlight rippling on the water!

The "*spectacle*[44]" does not leave him in the days to come. It troubles his thoughts – what might it mean? He has been shown something which he knows to be important, but he does not understand it – it reveals to him "*unknown modes of being*" (line 37). These, for the Romantics, are things that are in this world (physically, as the black peak clearly was) but which also suggest something beyond the merely physical, which could be called "spiritual" or "revelatory"; they tell us about our place in the world and our relationship to it. At the moment, the young Wordsworth has not worked out what this all means, exactly. His mind is a troubled "*blank*" (line 39)– aware that he has seen something important, but unable to process it. Look at how he gropes for words ("*call it*") to describe how he feels: "*darkness*", "*solitude*", "*desertion*". For a poet, his words failing him is bewildering.

His experience affects his whole outlook on the world around him – things are no longer as they once seemed. The surface of the everyday world to which he is accustomed, indicated by the "*trees*", "*sea, "sky" "fields*", is overlaid with an awareness of something "other" that exists alongside this, at times hidden (like the peak), at other times revealed to the mind of the poet. What this is, exactly, is left unresolved. Call it "*the power of imagination*", call it "*Nature*", "*the meaning of life*". At this point, Wordsworth is concerned with the recognition of something outside his daily, worldly experience, the meaning of which he will grapple as he grows to maturity as a man and a poet.

---

[43] "*covert*" means both a hiding place and secret.
[44] A *spectacle* is something dramatic that has been seen

My Last Duchess – Robert Browning

Context

This is the greatest poem in the whole cluster, and possibly (probably) one of the greatest poems ever written. It is certainly the greatest *dramatic monologue* - the one against which all other poems in this form are judged. A *dramatic monologue* is a poem where the poet takes on a *persona* - a character who is not himself - and speaks in his voice. However, that is not to say that the poet is entirely absent. The poet may refer to emotions, events or ideas which he has himself experienced, or be using the *persona* to debate topical questions of the day.

Browning delighted in exploring the minds of socio- and psychopaths: in other poems by him, *Porphyria's Lover* is a murderer; the woman in *The Laboratory* is planning to poison at least three of her rivals in love; the Duke of Ferrara in this poem has ordered a murder. His poems are often set in historical time periods; he also wrote *dramatic monologues* in the *personae* of Renaissance artists of the 14th century, such as Andrea del Sarto and Fillipo Lippi.

Browning's poem is based on the true story of the marriage between Alfonso, Duke of Ferrara, and Lucrezia de 'Medici in the 16th century. The background can be found in Wiki here: https://en.wikipedia.org/wiki/My_Last_Duchess There is a wealth of material on the web about this poem, as it is one of the most anthologised and studied.

Themes

The Victorian poets (of whom Browning is one) used the *dramatic monologue* to debate the position of women in society, sexual relationships and gender identity, the nature of work and finding purpose in life, religious doubt and societal ills, in their search to make sense of their lives in a world that was rapidly changing. The *dramatic monologue* allowed them the freedom to explore radical ideas without the fear of public censure. They were not always successful in the last - commentators of the day sometimes saw through the pretence and criticised them as scandalous.

In this poem, Browning seems more interested in the psychology of an individual man than he does in making any more general commentary on society in general. The Duke is a psychopath, arrogant and proud, and wielding unlimited power over his wife and his subjects. He has formed powerful alliances with other Dukedoms (hence the arrival of an ambassador from the *"Count"* to negotiate a dowry for his new bride). He sees nothing wrong in "removing" barriers to his own advancement and personal pleasure. The poem reveals, through the persona of the Duke, **power as corruptive** of individuals and of relationships and **exploitative of the weak**. In this, it can be linked to Armitage's *"Remains"*, which is also a *dramatic monologue*, in which the persona is a soldier who wields the power of life and death over his enemy and is **dehumanised** in the process. The photographer in Duffy's *"War Photographer"* also wields a kind of power over his "subjects" – he chooses whether their stories will be told, or not, through the pictures he takes. **Dehumanisation** is also a theme here, as the photographer "collects" photos of the victims of war rather as the Duke "collects" art objects. *"My Last Duchess"* also links to *"Ozymandias"* in its portrayal of a **powerful man's contempt** for those he rules, whom he commands to *"despair"*.

Form, Structure and Language

Poetry is an oral art form. It is the poet's voice - heard through the rhythm, the rhyme, *syntax* and punctuation, as well as the auditory poetic techniques - which lifts the words off the page and makes sense of them. To understand a *dramatic monologue*, you have to HEAR the voice. With the *dramatic monologue*, and Browning's in particular, you have to be sensitive to what the *persona* is NOT saying, as much as to what he IS saying. We hear Browning's views on his subject, and his subject matter, in the gaps. The technique which he uses most to create the cadence of the voice of the *persona* and reveals what he is actually like, as opposed to the version of himself that he gives the listener, is *enjambment* - running the sense of a line onto the next (giving emphasis to the first words of the succeeding line) and *caesura* - breaking or stopping in the middle of the line.

The frequent use of these techniques not only reveals to us the true story behind the persona's version of it, but allows the poem to flow, uninterrupted, for 55 lines, whilst maintaining a regular rhyme scheme of *rhyming couplets* (*aabbccdd*....), which is a technical feat in itself. Added to that, it is written in *iambic pentametre.* And yet, read with sensitive attention to the flow of the sense in relation to the lines, both the regularity of the rhyme and the rhythm go all but unnoticed. And where they are noticeable, there is a very good reason for them to be so. I strongly advise you to listen to a recording of this work and you could do worse than listen to this dramatised reading by Julian Glover, at www.youtube.com/watch?v=i5AoZY6a_kE which is not very good quality, but captures the subtleties, as does this one by the late actor James Mason: www.youtube.com/watch?v=_ZbNrNE9q8g. Just ignore the painting which accompanies the last - it is Victorian, not Renaissance, which is when Browning's poem is set.

My Last Duchess
Ferrara

That's my last Duchess painted on the wall,
Looking as if she were alive. I call
That piece a wonder, now; Fra Pandolf's hands
Worked busily a day, and there she stands.

First, note the pun in the title. Does *"Last"* here mean final, as in *"the last one I will ever have?"* or *"The last one in a continuing line"*? The answer is given in the poem, but forms part of the intrigue of the opening. The title is repeated in the first line, but immediately given a sinister overtone: *"looking as if she were alive."* This could be a reference to it being a *life-like* painting – or is it a reference to something else? The pride the Duke takes in the painting is evident – *"a wonder"* - so maybe he is simply reflecting on the skill of Fra Pandolf, the painter. Notice how the pattern of *enjambment* and *caesura* is set up, making the regular rhyme-scheme all but unnoticeable.

Will't please you sit and look at her? I said
"Fra Pandolf" by design, for never read
Strangers like you that pictured countenance,
The depth and passion of its earnest glance,
But to myself they turned (since none puts by
The curtain I have drawn for you, but I)
And seemed as they would ask me, if they durst,
How such a glance came there; so, not the first
Are you to turn and ask thus.

It now becomes evident that the Duke is not talking to the reader, but to an unseen listener, although the effect is to put us, the reader, in the place of the unseen listener. And it also becomes clear that this is not the first time that the Duke has shown the picture to a visitor, and their reaction to the painting has been similar – amazement at the *"depth and passion of its earnest glance"* – and they all ask the same question – *"how such a glance came there?"* The Duke's response is in some ways equivocal. He names the painter *"by design"*, as if to explain the artistry of the painting, and yet seems to take their question to refer to the Duchess's expression in real life. He also shows his pride of ownership (of JUST the painting?) in the assertion that nobody shows the painting to visitors, except him. It is his secret.

> *Sir, 'twas not*
> *Her husband's presence only, called that spot*
> *Of joy into the Duchess' cheek; perhaps*
> *Fra Pandolf chanced to say, "Her mantle laps*
> *Over my lady's wrist too much," or "Paint*
> *Must never hope to reproduce the faint*
> *Half-flush that dies along her throat."*

The use of *enjambment* between *"twas not"* and *"her husband"* is illustrative of Browning's use of the technique. Together with the *iambic* metre, the *syntax* and the comma, it forces the reader to put emphasis on *"husband"* and *"only"*, which then becomes the focus of his explanation – that he was not the sole focus of the Duchess's attention. He then goes on to give examples of the events that caused the *"spot/Of joy"*: comments from Fra Pandolf while she was sitting for her portrait. How are we meant to take these comments? As sexual innuendo or innocent chit-chat? Fra Pandolf presumably shows more of her wrist in the painting, as it has been covered by her cloak, as small wrists were a sign of beauty. He then declares himself inadequate to the task of reproducing the Duchess's blush – the *"faint/Half-flush"* – caused by his comment. Browning, on the other hand, is more than capable. He uses enjambment between *"faint/Half-flush"* placing the *spondee* **"Half-flush"** at the beginning of the line, giving both words equal weight. He then follows with three *iambs* - "that **dies**", "a-**long**", "her **throat**" – two strong beats giving way to a gradual weakening as the flush fades and our attention is drawn to where. Abruptly, as if we too have been guilty of staring, the Duke continues, with another *spondee*:

Such stuff
Was courtesy, she thought, and cause enough
For calling up that spot of joy.

His dismissive *"Such stuff"*, (note the *assonance* with *"flush"* for contrast) conveyed by the *spondee*, shows his displeasure with his Duchess's reaction to the painter's flattery, even though he acknowledges she thought of it as *"courtesy"* – politeness or gallantry.

She had
A heart—how shall I say? — too soon made glad,
Too easily impressed; she liked whate'er
She looked on, and her looks went everywhere.
Sir, 'twas all one!

The Duke's complaint against his Duchess now becomes more explicit. There are subtle clues as to how we are supposed to take his censure, first in the placing of the *"A heart"*. Having a heart is positive – but the Duke's posing of the rhetorical question and the qualifier *"too soon"* sounds the wrong note – how can you be made glad too easily? His re-iteration changes the meaning slightly, but towards the negative – *"too easily impressed"*. We learn that she looked favourably on everything and everyone – *"'twas all one!"* She did not discriminate. So what are we to think about the Duchess at this point? Too easily flattered? Embarrassed when she is paid a compliment? Easily pleased? Liking everybody? The Duke gives us some more examples of things that gave her pleasure – and which seem to annoy him:

My favour at her breast,
The dropping of the daylight in the West,
The bough of cherries some officious fool
Broke** in the **orch**ach **for** her, the **white mule
She rode with round the terrace—all and each
Would draw from her alike the approving speech,

91

Or blush, at least.

A *"favour"* is a love-token, flowers or a ribbon, given by a man to his beloved. This is what the Duke feels the Duchess should value above all. Browning's uses a greater lyricism, in contrast to the colloquial rhythms of the preceding lines, to suggest how we are to interpret the Duchess's response to the Duke's list. He uses alliteration on *"dropping"* and *"daylight"* to describe her love of the sunset. He contrasts the Duke's dismissive *"some officious fool"* with the image of the (innocent) gift of a *"bough of cherries"*, placing the *"Broke"* at the start of the line, to imitate the action of the breaking branch, and creating a *dactyl* (one heavy, two light beats) to place a further emphasis on *"orchard"*. He places emphasis on *"**white mule**"* - white the symbol of purity, a donkey echoing Christ's journey into Jerusalem. She rides it *"round the terrace"* – suggesting she is confined, or perhaps that the Duchess is little more than a child. The images are of the natural world, in contrast to the Duke's artificial, artful one and the lyricism is in contrast to the Duke's clipped dismissiveness – and increasing self-justification.

> *She thanked men—good! but thanked*
> *Somehow—I know not how—as if she ranked*
> **My gift** *of a* **nine-hund**red**-years-old name**
> *With* **anybody's gift.**

Browning's lyricism gives way to the self-justifying, true "voice" of the Duke and we hear what is really bothering him – that she was as pleased by the simple things in life – sunset, cherries, her white mule, pleasantries – as much as she was pleased by what he gave her – status, a title and a *"nine-hundred-years-old name."* Browning places the emphasis on *"**My gift**"*, again using *enjambment* and a *spondee* (two heavy beats) [45]at the start of

---

[45] A *spondee* is a metric foot of two heavy beats (**TUM-TUM**)

the line. The true extent of his self-absorption and egoism are made clear as he begins to lose control, his sense of outrage growing. The beat becomes insistently *iambic*:

> *Who'd* **stoop** *to* **blame**
> *This* **sort** *of* **tri***fling?* **Even** **had** *you* **skill**
> *In* **speech**—*which* **I** *have* **not**—*to* **make** *your* **will**
> *Quite* **clear** *to* **such** *an* **one**, *and* **say**, *"Just* **this**
> *Or* **that** *in* **you** *dis***gusts** *me;* **here** *you* **miss**,
> *Or* **there** *ex***ceed** *the* **mark**"—*and* **if** *she* **let**
> *Her***self** *be* **less***oned* **so**, *nor* **plain***ly* **set**
> *Her* **wits** *to* **yours**, *for***sooth**, *and* **made** *ex***cuse**—
> *E'en* **then** *would* **be** *some* **stoo***ping; and* **I** **choose**
> **Nev***er* **to** **stoop**.

The language becomes increasingly threatening: *"your will/Quite clear"*, *"disgusts"*, *"exceed the mark"*, *"lessoned"*. The climax comes with the repetition of *"stooping"* and *"stoop"*, with the breaking of the regular *iambic* lines with the *spondee* on *"**I choose**"* and the *trochee*[46] *(*heavy, light,*)* on *"**Nev**er/ to stoop"* following the *enjambment*. The full extent of the Duke's anger – and what he does to allay it - becomes clear, as he reveals himself to the listener.

> *"Oh, sir, she smiled, no doubt,*
> *Whene'er I passed her; but who passed without*
> *Much the same smile? This grew; I gave commands;*
> *Then* **all smiles stopped** *to***get***her.* **There** *she* **stands**
> *As* **if** *a***live**."

The regular *iambic* line gives way to a series of broken lines as the Duke reveals what he has done, conversationally. Browning uses a *spondee* to give sinister emphasis to the Duke's

---

[46] A *trochee* is a reverse *iamb* – heavy, light (**TUM** -ti)

admittance of murder "Then all **smiles stopped**". The meaning of his introductory words, *"as if alive"*, repeated here and placed chillingly at the beginning of the line, are now clear. He has had her murdered on his orders.

"Will't please you rise? We'll meet
The company below, then."

The reaction of the listener is to leap to his feet and head for the stairs – notice the abrupt transition to the listener and the placing of the *"then"* at the end of the sentence, as if the Duke has, for once, and only momentarily, lost the initiative. The Duke continues talking, seemingly unaware of the reaction his revelation has had on his audience.

                                        "I repeat,
The Count your master's known munificence
Is ample warrant that no just pretense
Of mine for dowry will be disallowed;
Though his fair daughter's self, as I avowed
At starting, is my object."

The Duke reverts to an earlier topic of conversation, as if the revelation just made can go unremarked. The reason for the listener's visit is made clear – he has come to broker a new marriage between his master, the Count, and the Duke. The *"last Duchess"* is, indeed, the latest in a chain. The Duke is asserting that he is sure his demand for a dowry for the girl (the bridal gift from a father to the future son-in-law) will be sufficiently generous although, he insists, the girl herself is what he wants – but the word *"object"* belies this. Browning is punning on *"object"* as in *"objective"* or goal, and *"object"* as *"thing"*. She is just a trophy to him.

                           "Nay, we'll go
Together down, sir. Notice Neptune, though,

Taming a sea-horse, thought a rarity,
Which Claus of Innsbruck cast in bronze for me!"

The envoy appears to make a further move to get away but is stayed by the Duke, shown by the *syntax* that places *"Together"* at the beginning of the line, – *"Nay, we'll go/Together down."* As they leave, the Duke points out another *"object"* (or *"objet d'art"* as Browning is punning) – a statue of Neptune, God of the Sea, taming a seahorse. This image is deliberately ambiguous. As God of the Sea, Neptune rode huge horses with the tails of fish, as depicted in classical art, as at: https://en.wikipedia.org/wiki/Neptune_(mythology)#/media/Fil e:Sousse_neptune.jpg

But to us, a seahorse is a tiny fish, conjuring up the image of a powerful man dominating a much weaker creature – just as the Duke has dominated, and ultimately killed, his Duchess. To the Duke, she was a possession to reflect his power and status, as much as the painting by a famous artist or a bronze by a famous sculptor.

The Charge of the Light Brigade - Alfred, Lord Tennyson

Context

Alfred Tennyson, First Baron Tennyson, was a favourite of Queen Victoria and poet laureate from 1850 until his death in 1892. Poet Laureate is a public appointment, in the gift of the monarch, which requires the holder to write poetry for certain state and national occasions. *"The Charge of the Light Brigade"* was written within six weeks of the Battle of Balaclava in 1854, an engagement in the Crimean War (1853-1856), during which the charge took place, and was published in the national newspaper *"The Enquirer"*. The charge is infamous for the loss of life, caused by transmitting confused orders. The Light Brigade, a lightly-armed and armoured cavalry unit of around 670 men, led by Lord Cardigan, instead of being sent to harass retreating Russians and stop them moving guns, was sent into an enclosed valley to storm a gun placement manned by the opposing Russian troops, which was heavily defended on all sides. More than 150 men were killed and another 122 wounded and 350 horses died or were destroyed afterwards. The poem praises the heroism of the cavalrymen whilst acknowledging, but not exploring, the "bungling" that led to the charge being ordered. The action prompted the French Marshall, Pierre Bosquet, to pronounce: *"C'est magnifique, mais ce n'est pas la guerre. C'est de la folie"*. ("It is magnificent, but it is not war. It is madness.")

The Crimean War was one of the earliest to be regularly reported by newspaper reporters and cameramen "in the field". News of events at the front reached Britain only three weeks later and it was the eye-witness account of William Howard Russell, reporting for the *Times,* that formed the basis for Tennyson's poem. This explains the comment that *"All the world wonder'd"*, as news of the engagement reached the public in an unprecedentedly short time. The circumstances surrounding the Charge were the subject of controversy in the newspapers, and in parliament, with accusations made on all sides as to who was responsible for the *"blunder"*, in which the lightly armoured Light Brigade (instead of the better equipped Heavy Brigade) were sent up against a fixed nest of Russian guns positioned at the head of a valley, protected on two sides by gun emplacements on the surrounding hills.

Themes

As poet laureate, it is perhaps unsurprising that Tennyson should write this poem as a *eulogy*[47] – a poem praising **heroism in conflict,** rather than openly criticising the decisions of those in charge. It is not entirely uncritical, however, of the decisions taken that led to the charge. There is a clear distinction made throughout, between those who gave the orders and those who carried them out, with the focus on the latter. In the original, the supposed source of the *"blunder"* was named as "Nolan", who carried the orders, but this was later anonymised by Tennyson to refocus on the men. There is also an ambiguity in the word *"wonder'd"*, which can indicate both awe and horror.

Although the circumstances of the charge are documented in some detail and the horror acknowledged, Tennyson's poem approaches the Light Brigade as a single, indivisible unit of war, with no focus on individual suffering. In this, it can be contrasted with the cold realities depicted by Owen in *"Exposure"*, or the brutality of Armitage's *"Remains"*, or the cynicism of Duffy's *"War Photographer"* or the visceral fear of Hughes's *"Bayonet Charge"*, which all take a much harsher attitude towards **the effects of conflict on the individual.**

---

[47]An *eulogy* is a poem of praise. Do not confuse with *elegy*, which is a poem for the dead.

Perhaps this reflects a more modern attitude to war, starting with Owen during the First World War and, generally, continuing ever since, with the rise of a more individualistic culture, less bound by conventions laid down by the State and Religion than in Tennyson's time, and the increasing power of the media to report on events in real time. **The role of the media in reporting Conflict**, is reflected in both Armitage's "*Remains*" and Duffy's "*War Photographer*".

Form, Structure and Language

Tennyson's *narrative poem* is unique in its use of rhythm, rhyme and *anaphora* to convey the mad charge of the light cavalry into the "*Valley of Death*". It is written in a regular *dactylic dimetre* – two stressed beats in each line, with each metric *foot* being a *dactyl* – **Tum**-*ti-ti*,[48] to represent the thunderous charge of the horses galloping. The frequent *repetition* and use of *full rhyme*[49] give further emphasis, propelling the verse forwards, whilst keeping it under tight control. Note that this *repetition* occurs at the end of lines as well as the beginning, giving frequent repetitions of rhymes. The middle lines of each stanza also rhyme with each other: "*hundred*", "*blunder'd*", "*thunder'd*", *wonder'd*", "*thunder'd*", "*wonder'd*", underpinning the dichotomy between the heroism of the action and the folly of it.

Each of the six sections of the poem are arranged as a single stanza – Tennyson simply adds to or reduces the number of lines in the stanza to accommodate the story he wants to tell. Section 1 describes the giving of the orders to charge; section 2 gives the men's unquestioning response to them; section 3 describes the charge into the Valley; section 4 describes the engagement with the enemy; section 5 shows the retreat back

---

[48] See the section on *Metre* at the end of this guide.
[49] Full rhyme is where the whole word rhymes with another, as in "*thunder'd/wonder'd*"

up the Valley; section 6 praises the men's heroism, addressing his national audience.

Section 1 establishes the circumstances for the charge, using the reported orders that created the confusion, although leaving the *"He"* unidentified. Tennyson originally attributed them to Captain Nolan who carried the orders, which originated from Lord Raglan, to Lord Lucan, who commanded the Cavalry. It was the identity of *"the guns"* that caused the confusion. The *"Valley of Death"* is a reference to Psalm 23: *"Even though I walk through the valley of the shadow of death, I will fear no evil"*. Here Tennyson substitutes the metaphoric *"valley"* for a real one.

Section 2 imagines the Unit's response – although aware of the "blunder", they accept their orders unquestioningly. This may be Tennyson writing with the benefit of hindsight; it is not clear that Lord Cardigan, who led the charge and survived, realised the error until after the event. However, it raises the patriotic tone and again places emphasis on the men rather than their leaders. Notice the use of the *anaphora* with *"Theirs"* placed forcefully at the beginning of lines 13 – 15 and mirrored by the regular full rhymes on *"reply"*, *"why"* and *"die"* at the end of each *end-stopped*[50] line.

Section 3 describes the positioning of the guns in the valley – lined up along the valley walls, so that the men become easy targets as they ride between them. Again, Tennyson uses the repeated *"Cannons"* at the start of the line to mimic the overwhelming firepower that confronted them. There is a rare use of enjambment at *"volley'd and thunder'd"* to focus attention on the sound imagery. He repeats the reference to

---

[50] *End-stopped* means that the meaning of the line is complete at the end of it; it is the opposite of *enjambment*, where the sense is carried over to the next line.

the Psalm and also introduces the image of Hell as a wide-open mouth, common in Anglo-Saxon and medieval *iconography*[51].

In **section 4,** the Light Brigade engage with the enemy, brandishing their swords which *"flash"* in the sun, the word suggesting both speed and ferocity. The juxtaposition of *"Sabring"* and *"gunners"* underlines the imbalance between the two forces, as does the word *"army"*, with the Light Cavalry outnumbered and "outgunned". *"All the world wonder'd"* is a comment on the remarks of the Commanders of the allied forces on the action during the events, but also shows that warfare at this time was moving into the modern age of reporters and cameramen – both of whom covered the war (see "**context**"). The scene is brought vividly to life in the use of verbs of violent action: *"Charging"*, ", *Plunged"*, *Reel'd"*, all opening the lines, and the alliterated *"Shatter'd and sunder'd"*. Their action was swift, ferocious and deadly. However, they do not come out unscathed. Triumph gives way to bitter realisation in the repetition of *"Then they rode back, but **not/Not** the six hundred."*

Section 5 tracks the unit's return up the valley, the cannons still raining death and destruction upon them. The stanza is almost a repetition of section 3, but altered to show the terrible toll of death. *"Boldly they rode and well"* gives way to the alliterated *"While horse and hero fell."* But some escape the *"jaws of Death"* – *"all that was left of them"* – which is, of course, a miracle, in religious symbolism.

Section 6 gives way to Tennyson's praise of the Light Brigade with a rhetorical question addressed to the public reader and the repetition of the opinion that this was an event that was of world-importance, not just an act of heroism and gallantry of importance to the British. Line 53 is an exhortation to the public to *"Honour...!"* these men and their heroic deed.

---

[51] *Iconography* means pictures or symbols

The poem is often taken as an uncritical response to the Charge, portraying it as an unquestioning salute to heroic sacrifice for Queen and Country. Whilst it celebrates the bravery of the Brigade, however, it is not without an oblique commentary on those who, whether through negligence or simple error, caused it to happen.

Exposure – Wilfred Owen

Context

A popular contemporary saying about World War 1 was *"We went to war with Rupert Brooke and came home with Siegfried Sassoon"*, a comment on the length of the war itself (1914-18), the number of poets that flourished during the period and the changing attitudes to the War that their poetry expresses. In temperament, the early War poets were more aligned to Tennyson than to Owen or Sassoon; Rupert Brooke's *"The Soldier"* sees dying for one's country as a patriotic adventure:

"That there's some corner of a foreign field
That is forever England".

When the war that was supposed to be *"over by Christmas"* dragged on into its third year, attitudes at home and in the trenches changed, with public criticism of the decisions being taken by the Military, and the increasingly heavy loss of life. Most of Owen's poetry was written between 1917 – 1918 and published posthumously. He was encouraged to write by the poet Siegfried Sassoon, whom he met whilst convalescing at Craiglockhart Hospital following a diagnosis of shell shock - what we would now identify as Post Traumatic Stress Disorder or PTSD. Having returned to the front-line, he was killed a week before the Armistice, which ended the war in November 1918.

Themes

In the preface to his proposed first collection of poetry, Owen wrote:

This book is not about heroes. English poetry is not yet fit to speak of them.

Nor is it about deeds, or lands, nor anything about glory,
honour, might, majesty, dominion, or power, except War.
Above all I am not concerned with Poetry.
My subject is War, and the pity of War.
The Poetry is in the pity.

The title, *"Exposure"*, refers both to the men's exposure to the elements, which form a major part of the description of the hardships they face, to the effect of that exposure, which is death, and to Owen's own purpose in writing – to expose, or show, the horrors of the War to the public back at home.

Wilfred Owen was a soldier on the front-line, as were many of the poets, and documented the appalling conditions in the trenches, and **the effect of conflict on the individual soldier**, whilst asking the question "What is this all for?" The question is shared by Tennyson (*"The whole world wonder'd"*). It occurs also in *"Bayonet Charge"* when the soldier asks *"in what cold clockwork of the stars...was he the hand?"* In Owen's documentation of the individual human experience, his poem is close to Armitage's interpretation of the effects of war in *"Remains"*, or Duffy's in *"War Photographer"* which both suggest that the survivors suffer from PTSD – unknown in Owen's time, when it was called "shell-shock".

The poem is also notable for the use of *pathetic fallacy[52]*. Owen's poems often suggest that it is the whole world that is "out of joint" as a result of the War; **Nature itself has become hostile** and unpredictable and is oblivious to human suffering, whilst God is absent entirely. This **enmity between Man and Nature** has echoes in Wordsworth's *"The Prelude"* and, particularly, Heaney's *"Storm on the Island."*

---

[52]*Pathetic fallacy* (literally *"false feeling"*) describes weather or landscape as if it is in sympathy with the human subject of the poem. For example, wet and cold when he is miserable, sunny when happy.

Form, Structure and Language

The poem is written predominantly in *hexametres,* lines with six stressed beats, with some variation in the metrical pattern. These long, faltering lines can be compared with the urgency of the regular *dimetres* of Tennyson's poem which reflect the headlong charge, whereas Owen's men are held in a nightmare where *"nothing happens".* There is a regular rhyming pattern of *abba,* but instead of full rhymes, Owen uses *pararhyme,* changing the vowels whilst retaining a similar pattern of consonants in the final words on the line, again suggesting that the world is no longer held together by any rational thought: *knive us/nervous; silent/salient; wire/war; brambles/rumbles.* There is a recurring structural feature in the short *refrain* with which each stanza ends, which asks and answers Owen's questions about the purpose of this War, in an endless cycle:

But nothing happens
What are we doing here?
Is it that we are dying?
We turn back to our dying
For love of God seems dying
But nothing happens.

Throughout, Owen uses extensive *alliteration, sibilance* and *assonance* to evoke the sights and sounds around him, as well as *metaphor* and *simile.*

The opening stanza sets the tone of the whole – a nightmare world in which the *personified* cold weather takes on substance and attacks (*"knives"*) the men, both physically and mentally, as they await the next stage in the battle – which fails to come. This was a familiar pattern of warfare in the trenches – long periods of inactivity followed by brief and bloody engagements, similar to the sudden charge the soldier makes in *"Bayonet*

104

Charge". The men, although tired, cannot sleep, as the silence brings a mounting tension about what might be about to happen, as signified by the whispering lookouts, their anxiety conveyed by the *listing "whisper, curious, nervous."*

In the second stanza, Owen deepens the nightmare by using a *simile*, likening the wind buffeting the entanglements of barbed wire to the movements caused by men caught up in it while crossing no-man's-land. The distortion of nature is emphasised by the *metaphor* for the wire as *"brambles"*. The men seem detached from the real world – the sound of guns *"Far off"* seems to have no relevance to their situation, isolated in the cold silence around them.

Dawn-break beings no respite; instead, it begins to rain heavily. The *"melancholy army"* is a *metaphor* for the banks of storm clouds that move in from the east, again depicting Nature, as well as man, being at war with the men shivering below. Owen uses *hypallage* here, or a *transferred epithet*; it is the men *"shivering"* rather than the clouds that bring the cold rain, but the transfer from one to the other binds the two together in this misery.

Stanza 4 opens with a flurry of activity, the whistle of streaking bullets conveyed by the sibilant "s" in *"Sudden /successive /flights /bullets/streak /silence"*. But it is a false alarm. The bullets do no more, or less, than the snow which has begun to fall around them. Again, notice the use of *hypallage* with *"shudders"*, transferred to the snow-filled air from the shivering men below. The snowflakes (note the alliterated *"flowing/flakes/flocks"*) swirl around apparently aimlessly like great *"flocks"* of birds. Owen may well be thinking of the evening flights of starlings that create intricate patterns in the sky as they flock in their thousands, moving together, pausing and changing direction, the reasons for which we cannot understand. The wind is *"nonchalant"* (casual), without purpose, like the waiting men.

As the snow deepens in stanza 5, the men begin to suffer from the effects of *exposure* – they feel drowsy and the snow begins to feel warm as their body temperature drops. The snow is *personified* as the icy fingers of Death. They begin to hallucinate – are they now feeling the spring sun, surrounded by the blossoms falling from trees, disturbed by a feeding blackbird hunting for insects, as it did at home in England? Their vision of home, and their growing lassitude[53], is beautifully and intensely realised in the repeated *"l"* sounds: *"Littered/blossoms/trickling/blackbird"*. Unable to rouse themselves, they wonder, helplessly, if they are dying.

In stanza 6, the realisation of impending death "drags" them further home to deserted houses where once they lived. They are near-abandoned – the fires have been allowed to sink to embers and crickets and mice have taken over. They cannot go back – they are fast becoming ghosts in reality, but they have already become ghosts to those left behind. This is another recurring Owen theme – that, if not forgotten, the men sent to the front quickly became "ghosts" to wives and sweethearts, as if they were already dead. This image is also present in *"War Photographer"*, where the dead man whose photo he has taken emerges in the developing tank as a *"half-formed ghost"*.

There is a terrible poignancy and helplessness in the *repetition* at the end of *"all closed; on us the doors are closed"*[54]. All that is left to them is to endure and die.

Stanza seven reflects on the men's feelings about the cause for which they are dying. They believe that only by dying can those at home be saved; *"kind fires"* is *metonomy*[55], using a feature of

---

[53] *Lassitude* means lack of energy or purpose
[54] This type of repetition is called *epistrophe* and is the opposite of *anaphora,* where the first words of a phrase or clause are repeated.

something to indicate the thing itself. So, *"kind fires"* is a substitute expression for the home and those who live within it. Only through the soldiers' deaths can those at home live happily under a *"true"* sun – a way of life that opposes the oppressor (the Germans) whose political aims precipitated the war. The soldiers are afraid that God will not come to save their loved ones and their way of life – they are *"made afraid"* in their love. So, they are willing (*"not loath"*) to endure the suffering in the trenches; it makes them *"born"* again, even if their faith in God, and God's love for them, seems to be *"dying"*.

This is a radical statement for Owen to make; although belief in a God was already on the wane before the War, there is little doubt that after it, Britain's move towards a more secular society was accelerated. In the time between The Crimean War and the Great War, methods of communication had advanced significantly and news, together with postcards and letters from soldiers, were being brought back from the Front in a matter of hours and days, together with photographs of the widespread destruction caused by the heavy shelling of towns and villages in Flanders and the Somme. Support for the war waned throughout 1917-18 as the death toll rose higher. Many peoples' belief in a benevolent God, in the face of such loss of life, was severely tested.

The final stanza returns to the harsh realities of the men's situation and the prospect of death from freezing arriving in the night. Owen shifts the tense from the present to the future, imagining the patrols that will go out in the morning to bury the dead with their *"picks and shovels"*. Notice the positioning of *"Pause"* at the beginning of line 38 to give it emphasis and create a "pause". The images of the dead men are deliberately graphic: *"shrivelling/ puckering/crisp/eyes are ice"* as he unflinchingly recalls the frozen dead men that he himself has

---

[55] *Metonomy* can also be illustrated by the use of the term *"Golden Arches"* for *"MacDonald's"*.

seen. The final image of the *"eyes as ice"* suggests that their eyes were open as they watched their death approach, the clear liquid in the eyes frozen solid.

The poem ends with the refrain *"But nothing happens"*. This has multiple implications. There has been no engagement – they are still waiting; nothing happens as the patrols go out – the men are dead and beyond help; there are no consequences from their death – nothing happens to end the war and it drags on.

Storm on the Island – Seamus Heaney

Context

Heaney was born in County Derry, Northern Ireland, to a Catholic family and was the eldest of nine children, one of whom was killed at the age of four in a car-accident. His father and grandfather were farmers and a recurring theme in Heaney's poetry (although not here) is his awareness, and guilt, that he did not follow in his father's footsteps but became a poet and academic. He attended Queen's University, Belfast, but spent the latter part of his life in Dublin. He is one of the heavy-weight hitters in this collection, one of the finest poets of the 20th century, Nobel Laureate, Oxford Professor of Poetry and winner, in 2006, of the TS Eliot poetry prize.

This poem, whilst most obviously describing a literal storm on an island, is often taken as a *metaphor* for the long-running conflict between Northern Island and the Republic of Ireland, making "Island" a pun. It has also been pointed out that letters from the opening three words spell "*Storm-on -t*", *Stormont*, previously the home of the Parliament of Northern Ireland, until it came under Direct Rule in 1972, and since 1998, the location of the Northern Ireland Assembly, formed on the conclusion of the 1998 Good Friday Agreement.

The poem was included in Heaney's first published book of poetry "*Death of a Naturalist*" in 1966, so any comment on the politics of Northern Ireland must be a reference to the growing tensions between the Protestant majority and Catholic minority leading up to the period between 1968 and 1998, euphemistically known as the "Troubles". Sectarian violence during the Troubles resulted in suspension of the Parliament and Direct Rule from London, British troops on the streets of Belfast, 3600 killed and 50,000 injured.

Themes

Taking the literal meaning first, the poet depicts **the power of nature** but also, paradoxically, **its impotence**. Man is *"prepared"*; he can survive this, by hunkering down and waiting for the storm to pass, even though at the time it appears fearsome. A storm can have an effect on the landscape over which it passes and its inhabitants, but it will pass. Perhaps being born and brought up on a farm gives Heaney a practical outlook on extremes of weather. **Nature may have enmity towards man**, as in Owen's *"Exposure"*, but Heaney's message is focused on man's survival rather than death. However, there are echoes of Wordsworth's *"unknown modes of being"* in that the poem ends on a paradox – a contradiction. Heaney describes the storm as a *"huge nothing"* – it is merely air moving very fast. Even so, it is feared, irrationally, by those that it passes over.

It is these last lines that suggest that the poem is not without political or social comment. Heaney seems to suggest that the tensions ("storms") between the Catholic minority and Protestant majority, although ostensibly about the former's desire to become part of the Republic and the latter's wish to stay part of the United Kingdom, can be reduced to no more than an irrational **fear of *"the other"*** – fear of people they perceive to be not like them. This has become known as *"Othering"* and is high on the current political, post-Brexit/post-Trump agenda once again. However, the islanders *"preparedness"* in the face of the storm suggests that Heaney believed, optimistically, that the citizens of Ireland would weather the political turmoil and win through in the end – which indeed was proved to be true with the signing of the Agreement, but not without considerable hardship faced on both sides.

Form, Structure and Language

Wordsworth was one of the major poetic influences on Heaney and both share a love of describing their observations of the natural world in intricate detail whilst drawing wider inferences from it. Much of Heaney's early poetry is rooted in his observations of nature whilst growing up on his father's farm. The natural world teaches the poet how to think about his life and his relationship to the world and to others who live within it.

The poem is written in a single stanza of *blank verse* – lines of unrhymed *iambic pentametre,* as is *"The Prelude"*. This gives the poem a kind of solidity that suits his subject matter – the islanders hunkering down in their well-built houses to sit out the coming storm.

The poem could be (and has been) described as a *dramatic monologue*, with Heaney taking on the persona of an island dweller, which would give plausibility to the idea of the whole being a *metaphor*, as Heaney was not known for being an islander. However, the voice is so unmistakably Heaney's, with its frequent use of *enjambment* and *caesura* to create a fluid, conversational tone and to guide the reader through the argument, that it seems to add little to our appreciation of the poem to assume that it is not Heaney describing his own experience of a storm, whilst allowing it to broaden out to a more universal *"We"* to suggest a *metaphor*. In this, he can be contrasted with Owen in *"Exposure"*, whose focus is on the experience of the individual.

The poem opens *in media res*[56] with a blunt statement of readiness and defiance in the face of the coming storm. This has been happening for generations; their houses are built in readiness of local, natural materials suited to the environment:

---

[56] *In media res* means "in the middle of events"

111

"*rock*" and "*slate*". Notice the positioning of "*Sink*" at the beginning of the line, similar to Wordsworth's positioning of verbs for emphasis, and effectively "sinking" the house in the line. The islanders have adapted to their harsh environment on what is a bare rock, with too little soil to grow grass, so there is nothing fragile to be blown away by the wind. There are no trees on this island either. Here, Heaney's conversational, confiding narrative voice is heard in the use of the *enjambment* and *caesura* on: "*blows full/Blast; you know what I mean – *".

He goes on to suggest that the islanders could, if they had trees, draw some small comfort from listening to the wind wailing through them, deflecting them from their own worries. The "*tragic chorus*" is a reference to Ancient Greek plays where the Chorus comments on the events taking place and always knows the outcome of the drama. But whereas the Greek chorus remained outside the drama, the islanders are part of it; "*Forgetting it pummels your house too*" suggests that, metaphorically, the storm brewing over Ireland affects everyone.

Comfort cannot be found in the sea either. Heaney uses the *oxymoron*[57] "*exploding comfortably*" to describe the familiar motions of the sea as it breaks against the cliffs. He uses the *simile* of the "*tame cat/Turned savage*" to show how the sea becomes violent as the storm rises and seems to threaten the islanders. The sea for an island people is a defence against enemies; it seems that Heaney is saying that this is no longer to be relied on as the islanders/Ireland are battered by the storm of rising sectarian violence. Perhaps it is too fanciful to suggest that the sea is an image of the UK Government, who, in an attempt to control the violence, eventually shut down the Northern Island Parliament, instigated Direct Rule from Westminster and sent in British troops to keep the peace, a few

---

[57] An *oxymoron* juxtaposes two words or ideas that contradict one another, as in "*bitter sweet*"

years after this poem was written. The islanders' response is to "*sit tight*" and weather the storm as it attacks them. Notice the imagery of war in "*dives/And strafes*", "*salvo*", "*bombarded*", again supporting the *metaphor* of the looming Troubles.

The poem ends with a meditative "*Strange*", as if the idea of a storm being nothing tangible, merely a wind, has just occurred to him. These final lines are probably a reference to President Franklin D Roosevelt's 1933 inaugural address in which he asserted: *"The only thing we have to fear is fear itself — nameless, unreasoning, unjustified terror which paralyzes needed efforts to convert retreat into advance."* This address was given during the Depression, when America was facing severe economic hardship, and heralded the New Deal which put America back to work on a nation-wide programme of infrastructure building. It is possible that Heaney is using this reference as a comment on the need for the Irish on both sides of the divide to face up to their fears of one another and to put aside religious and territorial differences, which are "*nothing*", as neither are tangible – both are constructs made by people, - in contrast to the harsh reality of life lived on the island/Ireland.

Bayonet Charge – Ted Hughes

Context

Ted Hughes spent his childhood in Yorkshire and is best known for his poetry about the natural world. The subjects of his poems are often animals and birds as well as man's relationship to them and their environment. This poem is taken from his first collection, *"Hawk in the Rain"*, published in 1957.

This is another poem set in the Great War and is probably based on the experiences of Hughes's uncle, Walt, and father, William, who survived the battles of Ypres and Gallipoli respectively. This poem seems to be set on the Western front, as it describes the feelings of a soldier ordered to attempt to take the enemy's position. It probably takes place relatively early in the war – there were very few hedges, or hares, left by the end, following four years of bombardment by heavy artillery. This would fit with the date of Ypres (1914-15) and descriptions of the terrain – wooded farmland with many hedges, and before trench warfare has become established.

Themes

Ted Hughes is clearly influenced by Wilfred Owen, with the same intense focus on **the response of the individual to the trauma of war**. The central emotion of this poem is overwhelming **fear,** which causes the man to forget all that has brought him to this point in his life. As in *"Exposure"*, this soldier also has a moment of questioning *"What [am I] doing here?"* This is in contrast to the cavalry men in *"The Charge of the Light Brigade"*, who notably do NOT ask *"Why?"*, reflecting the different time periods in which the two poems were written and the public forum for Tennyson's verse. The image of the dying hare **links the man to the natural world**, creating a bond between the two – both suffer from the war raging around them, in which they seem to be the innocent, and helpless, victims. As in Wordsworth's *"The Prelude"*, the naturalistic description of the world in which the human drama takes place develops into consideration of influences beyond this world, the *"cold clockwork of the stars"*, similar to Wordsworth's *"unknown modes of being"*.

Form, Structure and Language

This *narrative poem* is written in *free verse;* there is no regular rhythm or rhyme scheme. Like Heaney, and Wordsworth, Hughes makes extensive use of *enjambment* and *caesura* to guide the reader through his narrative, emphasising key words through positioning on the lines. The poem is in three stanzas, with the narrative arranged in three parts. Stanza 1 recounts the soldier's mindless race for the enemy line, in the hedge across the field; in stanza 2 , the soldier almost stops, his blind charge giving way to a dawning realisation of his situation and wonder at what he is doing there; in stanza 3, he is awoken from his "trance" by the sight of a wounded hare dying in front of him. He continues his charge, to escape the gunfire.

Stanza 1

Like Heaney's *"Storm on the Island"*, the poem opens *in media res* with the abrupt *"Suddenly"*. We can surmise that the soldier has been awaiting his orders, which he has now received, and to which he responds instinctively. Hughes vividly describes the soldier's discomfort, with the repeated *"raw/raw-seamed"*, the *"heavy"* sweat. The going is tough; he is slowed down by the rough ground as he heads for the hedge behind which the enemy is hiding and firing on the advancing men. He cannot see them – all he can see are the flashes of gunfire and hear the bullets as they pass him. Hughes personifies the flying bullets, using the *onomatopoeic "smacking"* to describe the violence of the bullets travelling through the air and the sound they make. The soldier is also weighed down by his rifle, which is useless as he runs, as he cannot fire it. The images of violence and feelings of helplessness are conveyed by the word "*smashed*".

Hughes description now turns inwards to the man's feelings. The patriotism that brought a tear to his eye when he heard the propaganda back in England, and which probably drove him to volunteer for the war (as many men did in the early years), gives way to a burning in his chest as he fights to draw in air as he runs flat-out for his objective. Notice the frequent use of participles in this stanza to indicate that this is happening here and now: "*running /stumbling /hearing /smacking /sweating*" and the absence of full stops; it is written as a series of subordinate clauses to show the continuous movement – until the last line -

Stanza 2

As if the burning in his chest awakens him from his mindless charge, the soldier "*almost stopped*", and asks himself the question "How did I get here and what am I doing?". The "*cold clockwork of the stars*" suggests a mechanistic universe, which is echoed by the machinations of the "*nations*" involved in the War. He is just another part of this machine. The reference to "*clockwork*" is to the theory put forward in the early 19th century to support the belief in a Creator; the complex design of creation demands that there be a designer, like a watch. This was overturned by Darwin's theory of natural selection some years later. "*Cold*" suggests heartless. Hughes further explores the soldier's psychological disorientation through the analogy of a man who awakens from sleep (looking back to the opening "*Suddenly*") and starts to run from a nameless terror that is following him. The running is conveyed by the long, unpunctuated lines and the repeated "*running*". The man listens to hear the footsteps of the thing behind him, and in doing this, the soldier nearly stops in mid-stride, like a statue. Note the use of *enjambment* to mimic his stopping in: "*his foot hung like/Statuary*" and the *caesura* in the middle of the line to

116

bring the reader up short and stop. Hughes restarts the soldier's action with *"Then the shot-slashed furrows"*, the monosyllabic and alliterated *"shot-slashed"* contrasting with the long lines, but Hughes delays the conclusion of the sentence by breaking it across the line and carrying it on to the next stanza.

Stanza 3

The stanza opens with the abrupt verb *"Threw"*, shifting the focus from the soldier to the dying hare on the ground in front of him. The hare has been shot and disabled; it can only move round in a circle. *"Flame"* is a reference to its yellow colour, but also to the vividness of the creature against the soil and to its life-force, which, like a flame, is about to flicker and die out. Hughes puns on the words *"Threshing"* and *"thrashing"* which are forms of the same word, originally both meaning to beat. A *"threshing circle"* was formed by farmers to beat the grains out of the wheatears, separating them for milling. Hares typically live in wheat fields. *"Thrashing"* is also used to mean a violent, uncontrolled movement, such as exhibited by the hare in its death throes. Hughes's detailed observation of animals is evident in his description of the hare's *"eyes standing out."* Hare's eyes are noticeably protuberant.

Aroused by this sight from his momentary hesitation, the soldier resumes his forward movement – convulsively, as indicated by the word *"plunged"*. It seems he has seen his probable death in the death of the hare. He has drawn his bayonet – the knife that protrudes from the end of a rifle, for use in close combat – and runs *"yelling"* towards the hedge. All his previous feelings of doing this for patriotic reasons have been left behind in his blind panic. The *"etcetera"* shows that these feelings are something that can be enjoyed when you are not staring death in the face. Survival becomes of paramount importance. All he wants to do is get out of the rifle fire, *"that blue crackling air"*, before his terror explodes within in him and he becomes as mindless and helpless as the threshing hare.

117

Remains – Simon Armitage

Context

Armitage presumably marks the break in the cluster between "*Poems Past*" and "*Poems Present*", as he is still alive, as are the poets that follow him in the anthology. However, this is largely meaningless, as poetry should be considered a continuum, with each generation of poets developing their art by reading, borrowing and learning from those that went before them. The context of the poems may change, but the techniques live on.

Armitage and Carol Ann Duffy, whose poetry is also in the cluster, are probably the most well-known poets today, partly due to their frequent anthologising by Exam boards, partly as both have public profiles – Armitage was appointed Oxford Professor of Poetry in 2015, Duffy is Poet Laurate. Their poems have similarities: both are often autobiographical; both reference the popular culture of their childhoods and of today; both draw on the literary poetic tradition to give layers of meaning to their poetry; both use a variety of forms and styles, particularly the *dramatic monologue*; both often write in an intimate, conversational style.

"*Remains*" is a poem from the anthology "*The Not Dead*" (2008) which originated in a Channel 4 documentary on the long-term effects on soldiers involved in conflict, based on interviews with the soldiers themselves. The whole programme can be listened to here: https://www.youtube.com/watch?v=MvA3K-tC6t8 and just the interview which gave rise to this poem here: https://www.youtube.com/watch?v=2DHWqppktFo

The poem reflects the experiences of a soldier in Basra, during the Iraq invasion and occupation by allied US and British troops between 2003 – 2007, which resulted in the overthrow of Saddam Hussain, the Iraqi dictator.

Themes

The title of the poem indicates one of the main themes. "*Remains*" means "what is left behind" and refers to both the remains of the dead looter, killed by the soldiers, and the aftermath of the incident on the mental health of the soldier. The poem explores the **long-term psychological effects** of exposure to violence, death and killing of soldiers involved in conflict – now known as *post-traumatic stress disorder* or *PTSD*. It shows **how combatants are also victims of conflict**, like the soldier in "*Bayonet Charge*" or the men in "*Exposure*". The predominant emotion of the soldier depicted is **Guilt,** which links the poem to "*Kamikaze*", as both combatants re-evaluate actions that they have taken under orders and have to live with their guilt, making them both combatants but also victims. The poem explores the **dehumanisation** of the individual when in extreme situations, as the soldier wields the power of life and death over his enemy and is **dehumanised** in the process. The soldier in "*Bayonet Charge*" is also **dehumanised** and reduced to mindless instinct when his life is threatened. The action of the three soldiers reveals **power as corruptive** of individuals and of relationships, and **exploitative of the weak,** which links it to "*My Last Duchess*" and **"*Ozymandias*".**

Form, Structure and Language

The poem is a *dramatic monologue*, the persona being a British soldier in occupied Basra, Iraq. Armitage uses the *vernacular* – the everyday speech – of the soldier to describe his experience. In fact, Armitage built his poem around the recorded words of the soldier interviewed for the documentary.

In spite of the poem seeming to use everyday speech, it is written in predominantly *tetrametres,* with four stressed beats in a line, but with a variety of metric patterns. Armitage also uses a variety of rhyming techniques, including *half-rhymes, assonance* and *consonance*[58] to make the poem more than merely a recorded narrative; it is highly crafted and controlled, and never loses the sound of the soldier's *idiolect*[59]. Armitage manipulates rhyme, line length and the structure of the stanzas to point up the disconnect between the horror of the events and the soldiers' reactions to it, at times with a grim, ironic humour.

The poem opens as if we have been listening to a soldier recalling various incidents during his tour of duty in Basra; this is to be another "peace-keeping" detail to stop looters, a recurring problem in cities ravaged by war where the forces of law and order have broken down. The use of the *vernacular* is evident in the expression *"legs it"*, meaning to run. The disconnect between the occupying forces and the civilians is evident in the casual *"possibly armed, possibly not"*; the soldiers don't really care either way. To them, the people of the town are a problem to be dealt with; the niceties of right and wrong, of *"proportionate response*[60]*"* mean very little in a war zone. Notice also the lack of solid information – the soldiers are sent out to deal with a problem with little intelligence to guide them – not unlike Tennyson's Light Brigade over a century earlier.

The conversational, casual tone continues in the next stanza with *"Well..."* and the grammatically incorrect *"myself"*. The repeated *"somebody else and somebody else"*, referring to the other members of his squad, shows that they are not responding as rational individuals, they are caught up in "group-think", a hive-mind; the process of dehumanisation has begun. They *"are all of the same mind"* and *"open fire"* without thinking through their actions or weighing up the options. The man is running away, (he too is *"fleeing"* like the bullets *"fly"*) but the implication of this has been lost to the soldiers.

---

[58] *Assonance* is rhyming vowels; *consonance* is rhyming consonants.
[59] *Idiolect* is the unique speech pattern of an individual
[60] *"proportionate response"* means using just enough force to contain the situation without risk to either side and without escalation.

The *enjambment* across the stanza: *"and I swear/ I see"* marks the transition from anecdote to unforgettable horror as he recalls what he *"sees"*, in gruesome detail. The effect of the three soldiers opening fire is beyond his imagining (hence the *"I swear"*, in case his audience does not believe it either), as the man is ripped apart by the bullets. This stanza is tightly controlled by the repeated *"I see"* and the *assonance* of *"life/aside/times/inside"* to focus on the soldier's description. At the end, words fail him: *"sort of inside out,"*.

It is Armitage's voice we hear at the start of stanza 4, giving words to the image: *"pain itself, the image of agony"*, which recalls Hughes's description of the dying hare in *"Bayonet Charge"*. We hear the soldier's voice again as he recounts the actions of his fellow squaddie, who *"tosses his guts back into his body"*. The casual language (*"mates"*) and action are in stark contrast to the reality of what is being done, the words *"tosses"* and *"carted"*, as if the dead man was a piece of meat, again showing the process of dehumanisation. The incongruity is also shown in Armitage's use of near-rhyme here: *"agony/goes by/body/lorry"* and *"story"* in the next stanza, so that we are in danger of skipping over the reality of the situation by the rhymes tripping along, just as the soldier believes that he too can make light of what he has witnessed.

But it is not the *"end of story"* for the soldier. The image of the man remains in his mind every time he sees the man's *"shadow"* marked in blood on the road. Note the elongated line length, as if echoing the image that recurs day after day *"on patrol"*. The image stays with him even when he returns home on leave. Armitage positions the *"blink"* at the end of the last line of the stanza to mark the sudden flash of memory, which catches him unawares and to transition unexpectedly to the memory itself.

Stanzas 6 recaps the incident, using the same words and phrases as in earlier stanzas, in an endless, looping film behind the man's eyes, whether he is awake or asleep. The memories lead him to try and numb the pain with *"drink or drugs"*, but they fail to *"flush him out"*, meaning both wash the man out of his brain, and the action the soldiers took to drive him out of the bank.

Stanza 7 shows the extent to which the dead man haunts the soldier. *"Dug in"* is a pun; soldiers "dig in" when they are establishing a position to await the enemy. This enemy has dug himself into his enemy's lines, the soldier's memory, and will not give up his position. He should have stayed dead in a *"distant"* land, Iraq being characterised negatively, and as very different from home, by the alliterated and sibilant *"sun-stunned/sand-smothered/desert sand"*. But this distance and difference is obliterated by the soldier's memories of the man.

The last stanza is cut short as he faces the reality of his on-going trauma. The man has not been *"left for dead"* nor buried *"six-feet-under"*; he is ever-present in the soldier's consciousness, and he holds on to the man's *"life"* as he did once before, but now unable to take the decision as to whether he lives or dies. The repeated *"bloody"* is both metaphorical – he has "blood on his hands", meaning he is responsible and guilty for the man's death – and also part of the soldier's *idiolect,* using *"bloody"* as a swear word of helpless exasperation. It may also be an allusion to Shakespeare's Lady Macbeth, who is haunted by the bloody murder of King Duncan. As she sleep-walks, she constantly rubs her hands, trying to "wash" away the blood, and cries: *"Out! damned spot! Out, I say! ...What, will these hands ne'er be clean?"*[61]

---

[61] Shakespeare *"Macbeth"* – Act V, sc. 1

Poppies – Jane Weir

Context

This poem was written as a contribution to a collection, called *"Exit Wounds"*, commissioned by Carol Ann Duffy, the Poet Laureate until 2019, and printed in *The Guardian* newspaper in 2009, just after Duffy took up her office. At the time, British troops were engaged in Afghanistan, where they had been since 2001, following the USA's declaration of war after the attack on the Twin Towers in New York on *9/11*. Duffy commented:

With the official inquiry into Iraq imminent and the war in Afghanistan returning dead teenagers to the streets of Wootton Bassett, I invited a range of my fellow poets to bear witness, each in their own way, to these matters of war.[62]

Weir's intention in writing the poem can be found in an interview she gave in 2010 here:
http://www.sheerpoetry.co.uk/gcse/jane-weir/poppies-jane-weir-interviewed-by-luca-brancati

The title *"Poppies"* inevitably recalls the First World War. Poppies prefer land which is regularly tilled for crop planting and, before the war, they grew in abundance in Flanders, where much of the War was fought. The constant upheaval to the land caused by shelling suited them well and they flourished even in the midst of the destruction. A famous poem of the War, by the Canadian, John McCrae, begins:

In Flanders field the poppies blow
Between the crosses, row on row

---

[62]https://www.theguardian.com/books/2009/jul/25/war-poetry-carol-ann-duffy

The poppy was adopted by the Royal British Legion as its symbol of Remembrance for its fundraising efforts in 1921.

Commentaries on Weir's poem show considerable confusion about the sequence of events, what exactly is happening, and when. Some commentators set the poem after the son has died, the farewell at the beginning said to be the mother seeing her son off to war and her visit to the cemetery as an act of remembrance that takes place after his death. But this cannot be right – the language and imagery does not support the idea of the boy, whom she bids farewell in the opening lines, being a young soldier. He is clearly a young child going off to, possibly, secondary school. There is no shift in time; the events take place in a single morning. The poem is an *analogy*[63] between bidding a son goodbye as he goes off to school and saying goodbye to a son going to war.

Jane Weir is a textile designer and draws on the *semantic field* [64]o f textiles for much of her imagery. She has two sons and acknowledges having the feelings expressed in the poem.

Themes

The overwhelming emotion in the poem is a feeling of **Loss,** and Weir explores this feeling through the relationship between a mother and her young son. The poem makes an *analogy* between the feeling of loss felt by a mother who parts from her son as he goes off to school, and also as he grows up and away from her, with those of a mother who loses her son to war. Whether this is a valid comparison, convincingly expressed through the poetry, is a matter of opinion. It is perhaps best to regard it rather like Heaney's poem *"Storm on the Island"*, being an account of an actual happening which can stand alone, whilst

---

[63] An *analogy* is a comparison for illustrative purposes
[64] A *"semantic field"* is the use of words all associated with a particular topic.

enabling the reader to draw wider inferences from it on the nature of loss in times of war and more generally.

Weir is reflecting on **the effect of conflict on the individual.** Weir has said that she was *"angry and frustrated at the apathy, or what I perceived as 'voicelessness' and ability to be heard or get any kind of justice."* Like in the *"War Photographer"*, the person affected is not a soldier, but a civilian. Similarly, in *"Kamikaze"*, the effects on the daughter and wife of the disgraced pilot are explored.

Form, Structure and Language

The poem is written in *free verse* and has been described by commentators as a *dramatic monologue*, as there is no internal evidence that the poet is also the narrator. However, there is also no apparent deliberate creation of a distinct and identifiable narrative voice which is different from the poet's and in interviews she has pinpointed the incident that inspired it – walking through a graveyard with her young son. The use of the imagery of textiles also identifies the speaker with the poet, Jane Weir. The tone of the whole is meditative and melancholy, with long lines like a prose poem.

The first stanza sets the poem firmly in time – it is *"three days"* before the commemoration of the end of the First World War and all other wars that followed, when poppies are sold for charity and decorate war-graves. The *"you"* of line 3 is not identified, but the use of the words *"lapel"*, *"bias binding"* and *"blazer"* all suggest that the person is wearing a school blazer, not a uniform jacket, which has neither lapels, nor bias binding (the ribbon sewn around the edges of jackets to protect them from wear) and is not called a blazer[65]. However, the words used to describe the act of pinning on the paper poppy are in the *semantic field* of conflict – *"spasms"* as of pain, *"red"*

---

[65] A *regimental blazer*, worn on formal occasions, does have lapels – but a soldier going to war would not be wearing one.

suggesting blood, *"blockade"* as in a military exercise, developing the *analogy*.

In stanza two, the suggestion that this is a child, not an adult about to go to war, is stronger. The actions of the mother, like the pinning of the poppy, are nurturing and over-protective. The mother cleans the cat hairs off his blazer; interferes with his collar which he has (perhaps defiantly?) turned up; at least she resists infantilising him by *"play[ing] at being Eskimos"* or mussing his hair. But the sense of the child beginning to break free of this parental (s)mothering is there, in the *"upturned"* collar and the *"gelled blackthorns of [his] hair"*. *"Blackthorns"* are bushes which have sharp thorns on them, signifying "do not touch", as the child resists his mother's control. Her feelings as she is about to wave her son off to school are complex. Weir uses another war image to show that the mother doesn't want her son to see that she is upset – she *"steels"* her face, turns it hard and expressionless. She finds herself unable to express her feelings in words, using imagery from textiles to show how her words become useless, like soft, formless, fabric. The *"melting"* is possibly a reference to her *"steel"* face revealing her true feelings, rather than the words.

In the third stanza, she rallies (*"was brave"*) as she lets the child out. The image of the *"treasure chest"* again suggests youthful excitement. It is an image from adventures in childhood – from the book *"Treasure Island"* with its pirates and treasure maps. The child bounds away, made drunk with the excitement of being set free – again, a youthful image not in keeping with the suggestions that this is a man going off to war. It expresses carefree, joyous excitement without any backward glance or regret.

The mother then goes into the child's bedroom. At this point, the *literal* (the real mother in a real bedroom with a bird in a cage) and the *analogous* become confusingly separated. It is hard to believe that a child actually keeps a songbird in a cage, so this must be a *symbol* for allowing the child (the "*songbird*") free of maternal control. Similarly, with the dove and the pear tree; both images are too trite (and unlikely) to be real – and shouldn't it be a partridge in a pear tree? The dove is (too?) obviously a symbol of peace. This imagery does not really work, because an analogy or symbol should illuminate the subject, adding to our understanding, rather than detracting. Instead, it is far from clear what is going on here.

Later that day, the mother follows the real (or symbolic) dove up to the cemetery by the church to stand by the war memorial. Her feelings of sorrow and loss are made physically evident by a "knot" in her stomach, which she again describes using the imagery of textiles, listing various types of stitching: "*tucks /darts /pleats*", which are all used to gather together material. She has given no thought to her own comfort. She has left her coat, hat and gloves, her guards against the weather, and by *analogy* her grief, behind. These are described in military language as "*reinforcements*", guarding her against the enemy of her sorrow.

The last stanza sees the mother reaching the war memorial on the hill, examining the names carved in it, and leaning against it, "*like a wishbone*". A "*wishbone*" is a bone like an inverted "Y", joined at the top, which forms part of the collarbone of a bird. Traditionally, the wishbone of edible birds, like turkeys, is "pulled" between two people, each grasping one side. When the bone snaps in two, the person left holding the small, joining bone at the top is the "winner" and can make a wish. She is likening herself to one half of the wishbone after it has been "pulled" apart, as she has been from her son, and cannot stand upright on her own, but has to lean against the memorial. This idea is reinforced as she watches the dove fly by, now an image of her son "*pull[ing] freely*" away from her, his separation from her further signified by the use of "*ornamental*" – the *stitch* now has no purpose, it cannot hold them together. As she stands there, she hopes to hear her son's voice carried up from the school playground to her on the wind, as a longed-for link between them, and a way of "*catching*" him back, as if he were a dropped "*stitch*". By *analogy*, the mother left behind after a son has gone to war might hope to receive a telegram or letter from the son who has been deployed to the front line, the "*playground*" being an *analogy* for the field of battle. This *analogy* between a school playground and a battlefield most famously occurs in the poem "*Vitai Lampada*" by Henry Newbolt (1862-1938), where cricket, played at his public school, was likened to a battle.

War Photographer – Carol Ann Duffy

Context

Carol Ann Duffy was the Poet Laureate between 2009 and 2019, the first woman to be appointed to the post. Like her predecessors, Tennyson and Hughes, she also writes for occasions of national importance, as when she commissioned the war poetry collection *"Exit Wounds"*. However, this poem was written in response to her friendship with a war photographer and is contained in one of her earlier collections *"Standing Female Nude"* (1985).

Duffy's poetry is frequently anthologised for students, on the basis, presumably, that being a modern author she is more "accessible" than poets of an earlier age. Unfortunately, this belief is erroneous. Much of Duffy's poetry is autobiographical, reflecting on her childhood, first in Glasgow and later in Stafford and frequently refers to the popular culture of her youth – the 1950s and 1960s. She assumes significant prior knowledge of this culture, which she uses to enrich her narrative. Similarly, Duffy writes in a strong literary tradition which harkens back to Shakespeare and the 17th century Metaphysical poets. Indeed, much of Duffy's poetry is Metaphysical in its use of *conceit* (a complex metaphor) and in her choice of verse forms, such as the *sonnet*. She also writes *dramatic monologues* in the persona of historical or literary figures, notably *"Salome"*, "[Miss] *Havisham"* and *"Anne Hathaway"* which lose much of their meaning without prior knowledge of their stories.

This poem explores the life of a war photographer, someone commissioned to take pictures in war zones, either by the Government or by newspapers. They are usually accompanied by a news reporter, if they do not write the copy themselves. Until recently, with the sectarian conflicts in the Middle East, members of the Press often lived charmed lives, being protected by various international conventions of warfare from

129

being targets. However, there have been a number of incidents within the past twenty years where these conventions have been ignored, resulting in kidnap and death for a number of journalists and photojournalists working on both sides of the conflicts.

Themes

This poem also explores **the impact of conflict on the individual**. Whereas other poems with this theme focus on people who are either combatants (*"Exposure"*, *"Bayonet Charge"*, *"Remains"*, *"Kamikaze"*) and/or victims (*"Storm on the Island"*, *"London"*, *"The Emigrée"*), this poem focuses on someone who is outside the conflict, looking in. However, it shows that these people cannot remain unaffected by the things they witness. The poem also touches on the **dehumanisation** of those exposed to on-going conflict and the **indifference** of people for whom the conflict is merely a distant event.

Form, Structure and Language

The tone of Duffy's poems is often conversational, intimate, following the rhythms of speech. However, this can be deceptive as they are also highly constructed. This poem is tightly structured in four stanzas, each of six lines, with a regular rhyming scheme *abbcdd*. This reflects the self-control and discipline of the war photographer, and his apparent detachment from his work. In spite of what he has seen, *"he has a job to do"*, which requires focus and dispassion. It his task to record and report, not to judge. His emotions are kept tightly under control. Duffy, however, keeps up a running commentary on his work, filling in the emotional blanks, as it were. Her attitude towards the photographer is not unkind, but it is less detached and, in places, deeply ironic. Notice how she uses *metaphor* and *allusion* to make her position clear. This is not the voice of the photographer that we are hearing in this poem, although she may be giving us a glimpse into his feelings - if he were to let his guard down.

The poem is set on the return of the war photographer from an assignment in a warzone. The location is not specified, nor does it matter; all wars are similar in causing pain and suffering, whether it be in *"Belfast"* (before and during the Troubles), *"Beirut"* (capital of Lebanon and the site of on-going conflict from the 1970s until the 1990s) or *"Phnom Penh"* (capital of Cambodia, a country torn by war since 1960s, and in particular during the "reign of terror" from 1975 – 1979, when an estimated 2 million people were executed by the ruling Khmer Rouge).

The man is in his darkroom developing the latest batch of photographs he has taken (this is pre-digital cameras and smartphones). The *"finally alone"* is a comment on the preceding weeks or months spent in a warzone surrounded by combatants and non-combatants. He now has time and space to review and sort through his pictures. Notice how Duffy uses the *alliterated metaphor "spools of suffering"* to describe them, and to comment ironically on the inability of these *"spools"* to actually capture real-life suffering. She establishes early on what is really going on here, and how she feels about it.

The photographer's apparent dispassion is conveyed by the ritualistic nature of his preparations, which she likens to those of a priest preparing for Mass. Duffy was brought up as a Catholic and shows her familiarity with the rites and procedures. The *"only light is red and softly glows"* is the red light used in the darkroom to protect the undeveloped film. It is likened to the red Sanctuary light that hangs in Catholic churches, to show the presence of the Blessed Sacrament, the wine and wafers that symbolise the body and blood of Christ given at the Eucharist during the Mass. It may also remind us of other red lights, as of explosions, that he has seen elsewhere and with an image of blood – both of victims and the blood of

Christ. His *"Mass"* intones a liturgy of warzones he has experienced around the world. She ends ironically with *"All flesh is grass"*, a quote from the book of Isiah in the Old Testament, meaning that everyone has to die, seemingly dismissing the individual suffering and sorrow captured on the *"spools"*. If we are all going to die anyway, why does it matter how, when or where?

Stanza 2 opens with the bald statement *"He has a job to do"* using the *caesura* of the line for emphasis – no room here for sentimentality or dwelling on the individual tragedies that unfold before him. However, *"Solutions slop"*, with its *alliteration* and *onomatopoeia,* suggest liquids that are hard to control, like the bodily fluids he no doubt saw spilling (and perhaps did try to stop *"beneath his hands"*?) from the wounded and of which he is now reminded, as his hands seem to be trembling *"now"*. However, he is back in the safety of England, his Home. But the echo of pain is conveyed in the *internal rhyme* Duffy uses: *"Home **again**/to ordinary **pain**"*, although this pain can be cured by a change in the weather. Duffy also contrasts the safety of England's *"fields"* with the dangers children in warzones are exposed to, by bombing and landmines. These lines may be a reference to a particularly harrowing picture of a child running between fields who has been burnt by napalm during the Vietnam war, which was wildly published in the media and is said to have led to the cessation of hostilities.

In stanza 3, as the photographer works, the negatives are gradually exposed to reveal a picture. Note the *parallel structure* with the first line of stanza 2 – the statement *"Something is happening"* and the *caesura*. He recalls the circumstances. Although he does not know the subject, he remembers the man's wife crying out as he sought her permission to photograph her husband. The word *"twist"* is used to suggest the uneven revealing of the picture in the solution, but also the grimace of pain on the man's face. He is a *"half-formed ghost"* as the picture is not yet clear, and he is only a faint memory in the man's mind. Also, the picture is the subject's *"ghost"*, he himself being, presumably, dead. So, in a sense, the photographer is not merely a priest saying Mass, he is also a Resurrectionist, bringing the dead back to life. There is an acknowledgement that *"someone must"* do this job – it is important not only to record what has happened, but also to give the dead a "voice". He recalls the man's blood seeping into the dusty ground, which is *"foreign"* to the photographer, being in another country. Linking with the references to *"England"* and *"Home"* in stanza 2, this could be an echo of the famous First World War poem *"The Soldier"* by Rupert Brooke (see the commentary on *"Exposure"*), but contrasting the photographer's ability to return home with the dead subject lying in the dust of his homeland.

Stanza 4 comments on the publication of the photographs in the media. The photographer will develop *"a hundred"* similar photos that capture the suffering of victims, to be picked over by his editor for publication. A *"Sunday supplement"* is a glossy insert to a national newspaper which tends to focus on photojournalism and is more light-weight in its coverage of serious news, often containing style and fashion articles. So, there is a suggestion that the newspaper does not take the subjects of his photos seriously – they are a diversion or entertainment and chosen for their shock value. Briefly, they will have an impact on the reader, bringing a sentimental tear to their eyes, but only in the space between getting up and getting on with their lives on a Sunday morning. Duffy's irony here is evident in the alliteration of *"bath"* and *"beers"* and the *internal rhyming* of *"tears"* with *"beers"*.

The war photographer heads off by plane to his next assignment, gazing down, apparently without emotion, at the countries below. There is some ambiguity in this last line.

"*Where he earns his living*" could be England, where his photographs are published and where he is paid, or the countries in the warzones where he takes his photographs. Similarly, the "*they*" could mean his English readers, or the people whom he is photographing. The latter "*do not care*" because they are too busy trying to stay alive to care about his job. Either way, the line shows the disconnect between those suffering and those reading about it, and how the war photographer treads a line between them.

Tissue – Imtiaz Dharker

Context

Imtiaz Dharker was born in Pakistan but came to England as a baby. She is another poet frequently anthologised for GCSE and appears regularly at *"Poetry Live"*, the annual reading of poetry by authors selected for inclusion in the GCSE syllabus. In 2014, she was awarded the Queen's Gold Medal for Poetry. As well as a poet, she is an artist, often drawing on paper in Indian ink and using text and she illustrates all her collections. Examples can be seen on her website. This love of paper as a medium of expression links her art to this poem.

Her poetry often reflects her multi-culturalism; born in a Muslim community she was brought up in Calvinist Scotland, first marrying an Indian man and later a Welshman and now spending her time between London and Bombay. This poem is taken from the 2006 collection *"The Terrorist at My Table"*.

Themes

It is not immediately clear why this poem is in this collection. It appears to have little to do with either Power or Conflict. However, the word *"Tissue"* has a variety of meanings which may give some indication as to what this poem is about. First, there is *"Tissue* [paper]*"* – a thin, semi-transparent, light-weight paper that is used where lightness, rather than strength, is needed. Second, *"tissue"* is what we are made of – collections of cells which together go to make up the various organs and parts of our bodies, including our skin. *"Tissue"* is used in a number of metaphorical ways – a *"tissue of lies"* means to weave together a number of falsehoods to make an apparent truth.

A link can be made with *"Ozymandias"* on the theme of Man's *hubris (*pride*)* in the face of **the power of Time,** which will ultimately destroy him and all his works – *"the shapes that pride can make."*. What endures, she appears to be saying, is the love between people and the memory of one another – which makes it arguably **a poem about the power of Love**. There is also a powerful image of light being allowed through a thin "tissue", and this light can be equated with the **power of Truth** – something which penetrates and transforms. Lastly, there are references in the poem to *"Maps"*, which can be seen as not merely marking physical boundaries on a piece of paper, but also determining **political and cultural divisions, a major source of conflict**. In this it can be linked to *"Emigrée"*.

Form, Structure and Language

The poem is written in a series of four-line stanzas in *free verse*, each exploring an idea, which begins with a consideration of the physical properties of paper and then, in a kind of *stream of consciousness*[66] links the tissue-thin paper to the thin outer skin of a person, possibly a lover.

The first stanza establishes the central *conceit*[67] of tissue paper and its properties which are then explored in the following stanzas. Tissue paper, being thin, is translucent, allowing light to pass through. Light is a recurring *metaphor* for truth or clarity in literature, and indeed, Dharker seems to confirm that her reference to light shining through does refer to truth, in that it *"could alter things"* – help people to see differently or more clearly and maybe lead to changing the world. This paper is *"thinned"*, made transparent, by the actions of people who use and cherish it. The tissue paper she refers to as an example is found in holy books, like the Koran, which are loved – *"smoothed and stroked"* – and are precious. It is also used to

---

[66] *Stream of consciousness* is a modernist technique in which thoughts are recorded without apparent editing or ordering.
[67] A *conceit* is a particularly complex or unusual metaphor. The term was first used to describe the imagery of the 17th century Metaphysical poets, such as Donne and Herbert.

store memories and family histories against the obliteration of Time.

In stanza 4, Dharker begins to consider the properties of paper and what would happen if paper were to be used in other ways. So, if buildings were made of paper, she might be able to see how insubstantial they really are, subject to the wind. *"Drift"* is a reference to the whiteness of both snow (as in *"snowdrift"*) and paper. She is suggesting that we only see buildings as solid and lasting because they are NOT made of something as flimsy as paper. This is the link to *"Ozymandias"* – he believed that his *"works"* would last forever, but he had no perspective of Time.

Dharker suggests in stanza 5 that *"Maps"* (which are sometimes made of a lightweight paper to reduce weight) are similarly considered by us to be fixed and unchanging, when in fact, they are just as mutable. When the light shines through, physical boundaries disappear, as the lines on the page cannot be seen. **The potential sources of conflict are removed**.

In stanza 6, this idea of things that govern our lives being insubstantial is developed with the image of receipts, the *"fine slips from grocery shops"*. Notice that this stanza syntactically follows on from stanza 5 (there is no full-stop at the end of stanza 5), suggesting that the governing clause is *"The sun shines through... Fine slips"*, just as it does through the *"Maps"*. Throughout our lives, we buy and sell, and nations buy and sell, the whole world caught up in a global marketplace. But in fact, these transactions are nothing. There seems to be a pun here on *"might fly"*. It could mean that they *"fly"* our lives as if we are the kites and they hold the strings; they are in control. But it seems more probable that it means we can make them *"fly [away]"* like kites, with us holding the strings, choosing whether or not to let them go.

Stanza 7 returns to the idea (in stanza 4) of building with paper, as an architect might do, piling paper on paper, some of it illustrated with text – as Dharker's drawings are. If he were to do this, he would never again wish to build with bricks, as building with tissue paper allows the light (of truth?) to break through the structures – the *"capitals and monoliths"*. These are the structures that make Man believe, in his pride (*hubris*), that he will endure for ever, like Ozymandias. But it is a lie.

Stanza 8 suggests that if an architect could build with tissue *paper,* then maybe he could build with *"living tissue"* – with human tissue, such as skin. This tells the "truth" about the human condition as human tissue was *"never meant to last"*. And human skin is like tissue paper when it is *"smoothed and stroked"*, cherished, and old, like the paper in the Koran in stanza 3.

The final line is deliberately set by itself, the word *"your"* transforming the poem from an abstract set of musings on the uses of tissue paper into something more deeply personal. In a sense, the poem should start here, as the transformation that takes place is from tissue paper into the lover's skin, through which the light of truth illuminates the meaning of life and which turns out to be the focus of the whole poem, as it is the only thing that matters in the here and now, revealing tjis to be a love poem.

This is undoubtedly a difficult poem; some critics have said it is unsatisfactorily obscure. However, sometimes poems do leave the reader with ambiguities. The Romantic poet Keats described this as *"negative capability"* or the ability *"to pursue a vision of artistic beauty even when it leads them into intellectual confusion and uncertainty"*.

The Emigrée – Carol Rumens

Context

Carol Rumens is a British poet and academic, born in South London. On her website, she says of herself: *"I would ... describe myself simply as someone who loves language, and who tries to make various things with it – poems, chiefly, but also essays, plays, translation, occasional fiction and journalistic odds and ends."* She writes the daily blog in *The Guardian* on the Poem of the Day. Rumens has made the literature of Central and Eastern Europe a particular interest, and translates from the Russian.

This dramatic monologue was written in 1993, placing it at the time of the break-up of Yugoslavia, which resulted in the Croatian War of Independence (1991 – 1995) and the Bosnian conflict (1992 – 1995). The former, particularly, resulted in the displacement of an estimated 500,000 people. However, Rumen leaves the identity of the emigrée's homeland unspecified, making it applicable to all displaced people who find themselves fleeing conflict, which gives it particular relevance for today with the flight of refugees from Syria.

Themes

The main theme is **the impact of conflict on the individual**, in this case a woman (*Emigrée* is the feminine form of the word) who is forced to flee her homeland as a child. The poem considers **the power of memory** to recreate the past as the woman rebuilds the city she left as a child in her imagination. It also considers **the importance of place in creating identity**. Unlike other poems which document victims' or combatants' negative experiences, and how conflict can dehumanise the individual, the "victim" in this poem is life-affirming and maintains her sense of identity, recreating her lost past.

Form, Structure and Language

The poem is written in *free verse* in three stanzas, two of eight lines and the last having nine. The additional line seems to build the negative forces crowding in on the girl, which she finally overcomes with the affirmation of *"sunlight"*, which is repeated at the end of each stanza.

The poem opens as if it were a fairy tale: *"There once..."*. Young girls are often the protagonists of fairy tales, as they are essentially "coming-of-age" stories where the girl-child faces dangers and challenges as she grows towards womanhood. The girl's memory of her childhood home is invariably positive; it is always sunny, even though she is told that it could grow cold in winter. There seems to be some significance in the naming of the month, *"November"*, linking it to a particular incident, which makes the cold weather a *metaphor* for conflict back at home, of which she receives "news". However, her image of the shining city is undiminished. She likens it to a *"paperweight"*. A paperweight is used to hold down papers. It is made of heavy glass and often contains intricate patterns made of blown glass or even real objects such as shells and flowers. She uses the image to suggest that the memory of her city grounds her, gives her a sense of identity, and that she holds within herself a clear image of it still. In spite of the conflict raging there, for her it is still filled with *"sunlight"*, so bright that it marks (*"brands"*) her forever.

In the second stanza, she finds that as the city grows more distant in time, her memories of it grow clearer. Even while she can imagine tanks rolling through the streets and the possibilities of returning become more remote, she is recreating the lost city. She uses the image of waters closing above her to show how she is becoming physically separated from it, if not imaginatively: *"rolls/rise/waves"*. However, even though she has been separated from her homeland, her native language is growing still within her. She brought with her a few words in her native tongue, but she is continuing to develop it, building a grammatical structure. *"coloured molecule"* is a reference to light, which is made up of a spectrum of colours. The image of the *"hollow doll"* again suggests that the poet is drawing on the culture of Russia and Eastern Europe, in recalling the "Matryoshka" nesting dolls. She is confident that she will be able to recreate it in its entirety, even though back at "home" it is now forbidden to speak it. She, however, cannot rid herself of it, likening it to a taste on her tongue, a punning reference to language being your *"mother tongue"*. Even this taste is like *"sunlight"*.

The third stanza expands the idea of being unable to return to her home. She is stateless, without a passport and so cannot go back. Instead, her city comes to her in memory and imagination, as if on its own *"plane"*. This image then morphs, first into the idea of it being a *"paper"* plane that lies before her, and then into a beloved doll, that she plays with. This "companion" then shows her itself – the *"shining"* city of her imagination which takes her *"dancing"*. She then seems to contrast **her** "city" – the sunlight bright place in her imagination – with the *"city of walls"*, which has been created by the conflict. The *personification* of this *"city of walls"* becomes increasingly menacing, the walls making a *"circle"* around her, enclosing her; accusing her of betrayal as she has left it behind; accusing her of *"being dark"* where it is *"free"* – even though she knows that it is still a conflict zone. **Her** city of the imagination *"hides behind her"*, as if seeking protection from a negative reality. *"They"* – the *"walls"* of the real city left behind and, by extension, the *"tyrants"* (from stanza 1, line 7) who now occupy it and have banned her language – threaten her with death, but she remains bathed in the sunlight of her remembered and imagined city, casting a shadow in front of her, attesting to its reality.

Rumen's poem, like Dharker's, requires the reader to grasp a central conceit – here the *"shining city"*, in Dharker's the *"tissue paper"* – and follow how it is used imaginatively to explore the poet's theme. This can be challenging and ultimately, the effectiveness of the poem depends on whether the struggle to grasp the meaning is worth the effort and adds to the overall experience of reading the poem.

Checking Out Me History – John Agard

Agard is another poet beloved of the GCSE Examining Boards and is a regular performer at "Poetry Live". Born in Guyana (formerly British Guiana) in the Caribbean, to a black father and white mother, Agard came to England as a young man in the 1970s and has lived here ever since. He is married to another well-known poet, also from Guyana, Grace Nicholls.

Agard's poetry is often concerned with the immigrant experience, particularly feelings of alienation from the culture of his adopted country, the experience of discrimination and the struggle of people of colour to have a voice in British society. He relentlessly writes his poetry in the *patois*[68] of the Caribbean, using dialect versions of English words, non-grammatical syntax and imitating non-standard pronunciation through his spelling. This is done with political intent; Agard uses his poetry as a form of political protest and activism. You can find a clip of him talking about the writing of this poem, which shows his proficiency as a *"performance poet"*, here: https://www.youtube.com/watch?v=LFV_06_UidI

The poem was published in an early volume called *"Get Back Pimple"* (1996), written for children and teenagers.

Themes

The poem is about the Euro-centric and revisionist nature of British history as taught in schools. It is **a poem of protest** and it explores the **conflict between the individual and society,** as does Blake in *"London"*, or Garland in *"Kamikaze"*, where the cultural norms of the majority exclude, or marginalise, those in the minority. This may also be regarded **as the abuse of power.** The poem also considers how **Identity is created through**

---

[68] *Patois* is the word given to various non-standard forms of English and French that originated, particularly, in the Caribbean.

language and a shared history. In this, the poem has similarities with *"The Emigrée"*.

Form, Structure and Language

The poem is designed to be read aloud, as are many of Agard's poems, so that the rhythms and rhymes of the *patois* in which they are written work together to create a kind of song. This link with music is made also with the recurring use of nursery rhyme words and rhythms, in the frequent repetition and the use of regular rhyming *quatrains*[69]. For the full effect, the poem also needs to be read in the dialect reproduced, in part, by the spelling and non-standard grammar.

Agard's argument is that Black history has largely been forgotten or suppressed, as historians and teachers were/are predominantly White Europeans who wrote history in their own image. In his discussion of the poem (see the link above), he gives the example of the colonisation of America, begun after Columbus, and the subsequent history of the United States which denies a place for the original inhabitants, the Native Americans.

The opening stanzas give examples of the kinds of "history" that British children are told. *"1066 and all dat"* is a reference to a popular children's book of the 1930s which, in fact, parodied history teaching by making ridiculous errors and misunderstandings about famous historical events. *"Dick Whittington"* is a London legend referring to the life of a 15th century merchant who became Lord Mayor of London, helped by his cat. He contrasts this abiding tale with the absence of any reference to *"Toussaint L'Ouverture"*, who was leader of the slave rebellion against the French in Haiti, an island in the Caribbean, in the late 18th century.

---

[69] A *quatrain* is four lines

In recounting this story, Agard uses features of *rap music*–extravagant and unusual rhymes overlaid on a regular beat, as in *"Napoleon/battalion"*, *"Republic born/Toussaint de thorn"*. This pattern of two "voices" – Agard railing against revisionist History (as indicated by the non-italicised printing) and his "new" songs or rhymes about Black historic figures (which are printed *italicised*) continues throughout.

Agard recounts other nursery rhymes that children are told, in an ironic comment on the merging of fact and fantasy that children learn. They hear about *"Hey Diddle, diddle, the cat and the fiddle"* but not about *"Nanny de maroon"*, or *"Queen Nanny"* who led a colony of escaped slaves in Jamaica during the 18th century. In recounting her story, Agard creates his own "nursery rhyme", telling of her vision of a free Maroon colony (*"see-far"*), which she created in the *"mountain"*. Her colony, called Nanny Town, was strategically situated on a bluff overlooking the Stony River (*"hopeful stream"*), making it impregnable. She would lead raiders down into the plantations, burning crops (*"fire-woman"*) and rescuing slaves to swell the free colony, which grew to around 1000 people, leading them to *"freedom river"*.

Agard continues to contrast what children are told with what is omitted from official histories: Nelson and the Battle of Waterloo (1815) but not the rule of Shaka who led the rise of the Zulu nation (1816-1828); Columbus "discovering" America in 1492 but not the fate of the native peoples – the Arawaks and Caribs, who lived in the Caribbean and were gradually killed or assimilated. He learns about Florence Nightingale, the pioneering nurse who practiced in the Crimean War (1853-1856), about the legendary Robin Hood, who stole from the rich to give to the poor, and even about the nursery rhyme figure Old King Cole. However, he does not learn about Mary Seacole (1805 – 1881), a Jamaican woman who also went out to nurse in the Crimean War, even after she was rejected for service by the

British Government. This *quatrain* in particular makes use of the rhymes to create an ironic humour: *"lamp/camp/soul/Seacole"*. Agard commemorates her achievements in another *"poem within a poem"*, this one more lyrical, particularly in the natural imagery of Seacole as a *"star"* and *"sunrise"* to the injured and dying soldiers, to counter the image of Florence Nightingale as *"the lady of lamp"*.

The poem ends with a repetition of the opening lines *"Dem tell me"*, reiterating the selective, and hence controlling, disclosure of information by those in power. Agard rejects this version of history, asserting that he will find his own and, in so doing, create his own unique identity as a Black man.

Kamikaze – Beatrice Garland

Context

Beatrice Garland is a full-time National Health Service clinician as well as a poet. Although she has been writing since 1989, she has published only one collection, *"The Invention of Fireworks"*, in 2013, from which this poem is taken. Another poem by her was chosen as the Unseen in the GCSE exam recently.

"Kamikaze" means *"divine wind"* in Japanese. Kamikaze pilots were suicide bombers who flew their aircraft, packed with explosives, into enemy targets during the closing stages of the Second World War, specifically the American fleet in the Pacific. The pilots were volunteers, apparently willing ones, who underwent special training, and many were young, student pilots. About 19 percent of pilots hit their targets. Nearly 4000 pilots died. The willingness to volunteer for these suicide missions has been attributed to the place of an "honourable death" in the Samurai (warrior) culture. Japanese military personnel were expected to die rather than suffer the ignominy of capture by an inferior enemy.

Although this poem seems to strive for authenticity, in the modes of narration chosen, by their very nature, *kamikaze* pilots did not come back. One who did, nine times, was eventually shot. *Kamikaze* pilots were instructed to abort for mechanical failure or changing military positions, but they were sent out again as soon as possible. The few survivors that exist, some of whom have been interviewed and their accounts found on the internet, aborted their missions due to mechanical failure and the war ended before they were able to go out again. This poem is an imaginative *"what if?"*.

Themes

Like *"Remains"* or *"Bayonet Charge"*, this poem can be seen as an exploration of **how combatants become victims** in times of conflict. No-one is unaffected. Just as the soldier in Armitage's *"Remains"* suffers for the rest of his life from flash-backs, so the pilot suffers the shame of returning alive from his mission and is shunned by his community. Feelings of **Guilt** form a large part of the on-going trauma – both men have broken a code, although the codes are very different. In this, the poem is also about **the tension between principles and duty in time of conflict** and are a contrast to the unquestioning response to duty by the *Light Brigade*.

The narrative is a recount of a story told by the daughter of the Kamikaze pilot, as she told it to her children. Four generations are cited – the pilot, his father, the pilot's daughter and her children – which suggests that **conflict affects generations** to come and casts a long shadow back into the past as well. In this, it is similar to *"The Emigrée"*.

Form, Structure and Language

The poem is written in six-line stanzas of *tetrametres* – four heavy stresses to a line. This gives it the sing-song rhythm of nursery rhymes, perhaps appropriate to telling a story, as the mother is to her children.

The first stanza reads as a third person narrative, telling the story of a father's role as a *kamikaze* pilot. This enables the poet to make an oblique comment on the story, with the benefit of a historic perspective and some irony. However, the mood shifts with the next four stanzas, which are written in one long, flowing sentence, and are ostensibly a recount of the pilot's daughter's story as she tells it *"later to her children"*. The final two (*italicised*) stanzas are in the voice of the daughter directly, talking about her experience growing up in the shadow of her father's disgrace. This structure strives to give an authenticity to the account, irrespective of historical accuracy and the poet's own feelings, about the pilot's actions and motivation. The poem ends with the daughter's reflection on the "sacrifice" her father made for his principles.

There is a difficulty, however, in that the central stanzas, which are ostensibly in the reported speech of the daughter (as it says *"but half way there, she thought, recounting..."* and then goes on to tell us, presumably, what *"she thought"*) are highly crafted poetry – quite obviously NOT the recount of the supposed narrator. There is a lot of poetic licence being taken.

The poem opens with an account of her father preparing for his suicide mission. Pilots did not actually carry swords in their planes; it is an imaginative way of referring to the code of honour that governed their actions. The *"powerful incantations"* are the brainwashing that young pilots underwent during their training to be *kamikaze,* here described as if they were magic spells. The comment *"one-way journey into history"* is an ironic one by the poet.

Just as the pilot decides to abort his mission *"half-way there"*, so Garland breaks her narrative across the stanza, beginning stanza 2 with *"but..."* and switching from her voice as commentator to the indirect speech of the daughter telling the story *"to her [own] children"*. With the daughter thinking about the moment her father decides to live rather than die, the poem becomes descriptive of the sea below him and the memories this stirs of his own childhood waiting for his fisherman father to return from a trip. There are a number of evocative images: the *simile* of the boats *"strung out like bunting"* (strings of flags); the vivid colour of the water with the *internal rhyme* "**blue**/trans**lu**cent"; the *simile* of the shoals of fish moving *"like a huge flag"*, their bellies *metaphorically "flashing silver"* in the sunlight as they turn upwards towards it.

In stanza four, memories of childhood return, when *"he and his brothers"* awaited their father's fishing boat.

In stanza 5, the italics indicate that this is the direct speech of the daughter to her children, in response to them asking if this was *"their grandfather"*, suggesting that this is an authentic account. The description of the boat is again highly descriptive, using the alliterated *"S"* in *"safe/shore/salt-sodden, awash"* to evoke the sound of the surf on the beach and a series of *noun-phrases* (a noun preceded by an adjective) to describe the catch: *"cloud-marked mackerel, black crabs, feathery prawns and loose silver of whitebait"*, the latter referring to the slippery, flowing catch pouring onto the deck, like silver coins. In contrast to these delicately described "small fry", she characterises the prize catch of a tuna, a large member of the swordfish family, as *"muscular, dangerous,"* perhaps suggesting the varied fortunes and risks of a fisherman's life. Fishing is also the work of a man who "goes out and comes back", in contrast to the expectation of his son, the *kamikaze*.

Stanza 6 continues the story in the direct speech of the daughter, as indicated by the *italics*. It describes the impact of what she experiences as a child growing up, as her father's perceived cowardice in breaking a code of honour (although the word is unspoken) results in him being shunned by his wife and the community. For a while, the children's attitude towards him is unchanged, but, as Garland indicates with the break in the stanza...

"til gradually" even the children fall silent under the weight of disapproval and they treat him as if he no longer existed. The final two lines revert to an indirect account of the daughter's tale, as she reflects on the "sacrifice" that her father has made and whether it would have been better for him to die a hero as a suicide bomber, or endure a living death ostracised by his friends and family.

Links, Connections, Comparisons and Tackling the Unseen Poem

Paper 2 - Section B – Comparison of two poems from the set texts

The exam question is in two parts. In Part 1, you are given one poem from the set texts (*"Love and Relationships"* and *"Conflict"*) and will be asked to choose another from the same collection with which to compare the poets' presentation of a *"theme"*. They will probably use the word *"Compare"*. Where possible, links and connections should be made to each poem throughout the essay, alternating between the two, for the highest marks. The examiners are less keen on one analysis followed by another, unless there is clear cross-referencing and/or there is a clearly comparative paragraph at the beginning and at the end.

There are various points of comparison that can be made. The Assessment Objectives examined are AO1, AO2 and AO3.

What is happening in the poem?

The first task is to understand *"What is happening in the poem?"* Unless you understand this, your analysis will be meaningless. Make sure you understand what the story, incident, event or imaginative idea is that has prompted the poet to write the poem. No poem exists in a vacuum – there is always a reason for writing it. Find that reason – the inspiration which leads to the poem.

The first "link or connection" to be made is to summarise, briefly, the "story" of each poem *and how this relates to the theme of the question*. This is the first response to *"How"* the poet has approached his subject. It is the framework around which he hangs his ideas. It is suggested that you do this in your first paragraph. It also reassures the Examiner that your analysis is not starting from an erroneous base. **Make the "story" the first point of comparison between the texts. What is the relevant context within which the whole poem is written? (AO3)**

Make any immediate comparisons of "**context**". Are the poems addressing the same themes but within **a different timeframe** (past/present, for example)? Is there any relevance of the theme to our **experience today which is different to theirs**? Are the poets writing in a particular **literary tradition**? What do you know about **the poets' lives** that is relevant and may be a cause for writing the poems? Are there any **specific events** that the poems are referring to?

Ensure that you always relate context back to the question. They do not want, for example, a history of Romantic poetry – but they do want you to show that you understand their **predominant concerns and styles** and **how this is reflected** in the poetry.

As you discuss **form, structure and language**, refer to any relevant **contextual factors that affect the choice of these elements**. For example, the use of classical or religious imagery reflecting a literary tradition or societal norms; use of language forms, such as dialect, that are used to convey the message of the poem.

Make relevant comparisons of "ideas", including your reactions to the poems and what you have learned from them about how people live or lived their lives, and how this relates to your own life.

Form, Structure and Language (AO2)

A poem may have many ideas in it. Your task is to explain **how the poet has used form, structure and language to explore the theme which is the focus of the question**. Below are some of the features of the poems that you can choose to explore, both when making links, connections and comparisons between the prescribed poem and one other from the *Poems Past and Present*, AND when linking the two Unseen poems.

Remember that the highest marks are given when the analysis of form, structure and language is related to meaning and to the theme under discussion. Fewer marks are given for merely identifying techniques in isolation from meaning. The commentaries on the poems show you how to do this.

It is important that you use *"examples"* (quotes) to illustrate your argument. Never make a comment about how the poet has approached his subject without an example to illustrate. You should also **never use a quote without then going on to talk about the quote** itself, analysing any structural or language features in depth and **relating this to the effect on the reader**. This ensures that you are covering the assessment objective AO2 – *"showing a critical understanding of the writer's craft."*

Section C – Unseen poetry is in two parts. There will be two Unseen poems given, linked by theme. The first question requires you to write about the presentation of this theme in the first poem given ONLY. Only AO1 and AO2 are examined.

Read through the poem, highlighting or underlining any poetic techniques that you can identify as you go. Read it through again, to ensure you have fully understood what is happening in the poem – the "story". Summarise this in no more than a couple of sentences, identifying the main techniques used and **relating it back to the question**. For example:

"The poet uses the *extended metaphor* of a "rope" to describe the ties that bind a mother and daughter together for life."

"The poet uses *nature imagery* to describe the love of the man and woman, suggesting that it is a natural desire."

"The poet uses *alliteration* and *onomatopoeia* to mimic the sounds of the man walking across the wasteland of his former home".

Then go through the poem from the top to the bottom picking out a few examples of the use of poetic techniques, in relation to the question, analysing how these techniques have been used.

The second question will ask you to **compare** the "methods" used by the poets to present the same, or a similar, theme in BOTH poems. By "methods" they mean "techniques" of form, structure and language. Only AO2 is examined, so do not waste time analysing the "story", or theorising on meaning, other than the opening couple of lines summarising what is happening.

Read through the second poem, highlighting any poetic techniques that you can identify as you go. Read it through again, making sure you have understood what is happening in the poem. Compare how the poets use the main techniques in each poem in relation to the questions. For example:

"Whereas poet A uses *natural imagery* to show the love of the two people, Poet B uses the *imagery of warfare* to show the couple's unhappiness."

"In Poem A, the poet uses a *regular rhyme scheme and rhyming couplets* to show that the two lovers are in harmony with each other. However, Poet B uses *free verse*, suggesting that their love is more uncertain."

"Both poets use an *extended metaphor* to describe the relationship between mothers and daughters. In Poem A, the umbilical cord becomes a "rope" which ties them together, whereas in Poem B, the mother describes her concerns for her daughter growing up as a Wargame."

Then go through Poem B picking out further uses of the techniques, linking them to similar, or dissimilar, techniques used in Poem A. Focus on the question and the techniques.

Note that the marks available for Section C as a whole are as many as for Section A and Section B. Section C is not something you can afford to leave until the last minute. Give yourself time to write a full answer.

Theme	The question will focus on a theme. Some key themes have been identified in the commentary on the texts. Choose poems which can be linked thematically as a first choice for linking, connecting and comparing. Trying to link poems "because you know them" is not a good plan.
Context	Is there a historical /biographical /literary /political/ social-economic background that is relevant to the text and the way it is written? **How does the context of the text relate to the meaning of the text and help us to understand it?**
Narrative Voice	Who is speaking in the poem? Is it the poet, or is he speaking through someone else? Is there more than one *voice*? The narrative voice is the person who is speaking in the poem. It may be the poet (many of the poems are autobiographical) or a *persona* – an imagined speaker, as in a *dramatic monologue*. Or it may be the poet simply talking to us about an idea that he/she wishes to explore. **What does the choice of narrative voice tell us about the poet's approach to his theme or about the theme itself?**
Form	Is the poem written in a named poetic form, such as *sonnet, ode, elegy, ballad*? **What does the choice of form tell you about the subject matter or the attitude of the poet?**
Structure	How many lines are there in a stanza? How is the story arranged around these lines? What is the subject matter of each stanza? In what order has the story or happening been told to us? Are there shifts in time or place? Is there a regular rhythm? If so, what is this rhythm? Is there a regular rhyme scheme? Are *full rhymes, half-rhymes* and *eye-rhymes*

	used? Are the lines *end-stopped* – does the meaning follow the rhyme and complete at the end of each rhymed line? Does the poet use *enjambment* and *caesura* to vary the pace of the line and create a looser structure within a rigid one? What does this say about the subject matter or the poet's attitude to his subject? Is it in free verse, with no discernible regular rhyme or rhythm? How has the poet chosen where to end the lines? **How does the choice and use of structure relate to meaning and what is the effect on the reader?**
Language	Is the language formal or informal? Does it sound conversational, confiding, reminiscent, musing, purposeful…? What is the tone? Sorrowful, regretful, angry, puzzled, triumphant…? What is the proportion of *vernacular* (words of common speech) to Latinate (polysyllabic, Latin derivations, "difficult")? Is the language descriptive, factual, plain, colloquial …? Is the language literal, or does it have many *similes* and *metaphors*, or *personification*? What kinds of *imagery* are used? Religious, naturalistic, mechanistic…? Are there particular words used which are unusual? Archaic, dialect, slang …? **How does the choice and use of language relate to meaning and what is the effect on the reader?**

A Note on Metre

Rhythm in English Verse

Rhythm in English verse is dependent on the pattern of **stressed** and **unstressed** syllables, or beats, in a line. This is called **metre**. In the examples, the *stressed* beats are highlighted:

*"**Half** a league, **half** a league,*
***Half** a league **on**ward"*

*"An **expert**. He would **set** the **wing***
*And **fit** the **bright** steel-**pointed sock**."*

The name given to the pattern of rhythm in poetry - the **metre** - depends on **a)** the combination of *stressed* and *unstressed* beats in adjoining syllables (called the **feet**) and **b)** the number of **feet** in a line. If the pattern changes in a line, the predominant pattern is used to define it.

Metric feet *(singular "**foot**")*

Iamb – unstressed, stressed (ti-**TUM**). *"And **fit**/ the **bright**/ steel-**poin**/ted **sock**",* which is a regular *iambic* line. It is the most common *foot* found in English poetry.

Trochee – stressed, unstressed (**TUM**-ti). *"**Fell** some/**times** on/ the **pol**/ished **sod**;"* which is trochee, trochee, iamb, iamb

Spondee – stressed, stressed (**TUM-TUM**). *"**Much** the /**same** **smile**?/ This **grew**; I **gave** /com**mands**; "* which is *trochee, spondee, iamb, iamb, iamb.*

Dactyl – stressed, unstressed, unstressed (**TUM**-ti-ti). *"**Half** a league,/ **half** a league"* which is *dactyl, dactyl.* Another example of a *dactyl* is in the word *"Liverpool"*

Anapest – unstressed, unstressed, stressed (ti-ti-**TUM**) *"'Twas the **night/** before **Christ**/mas and **all**/through the **house**"* which is a regular *anapaestic* rhyme.

Amphibrach – unstressed, stressed, unstressed (ti-**TUM**-ti) as in *"to**ma**to/po**ta**to".* This is rarely found.

The numbers of *feet* in a line are called:

Trimetre – 3	*Hexametre - 6*
Tetrametre - 4	*Heptametre - 7*
Pentametre – 5	*Octametre – 8*

Metric Forms (given in order of prevalence)

Iambic pentametre – is the commonest metric form in English and comprises a *metric line* of *five iambic feet.* Variation is given by the use of other *feet,* which gives the verse the sound of natural speech rhythms. However, the *five foot, iambic pattern* is always underlying. **NOTE:** you will hear people describe *iambic pentametre* as containing ten unstressed/stressed *syllables.* This is not the case. **It has nothing to do with the number of *syllables*** – only the number and type of the *feet.* This example makes this clear:

*"To **be**,/ or **not/** to **be**,/ **that** is the/ **ques**tion____*

There are **eleven** syllables – the extra syllable given by the use of the *dactyl*: *"**that** is the...".* The trochee at the end (*"**ques**tion")* – ending on an unstressed syllable, is also known as a *feminine ending.*

Blank verse is unrhymed *iambic pentametre,* commonly used by Shakespeare. It is NOT poetry which has no rhythm and no rhyme. That is *free verse.*

Iambic tetrametre is four *iambic* beats in a line, as used by Heaney in *"Follower"*. Note how he varies the regular *iambic* pattern to create stresses on words for effect, whilst retaining the four *feet* in each line:

Sometimes/ he **rode**/ me **on**/ his **back**/
Dipping/ and **ris**/ing **to**/ his **plod**.

The varied rhythm mimics the father's movements as he carries his son on his shoulders.

Tetrametre – is also the rhythm of many nursery rhymes. We describe this as "sing-song" as it is common in songs and light verse:

*"***Hump**ty **Dump**ty **sat** on the **wall**
Humpty **Dump**ty **had** a great **fall**...*"*

The four-beat ***iambic tetrametre*** line may alternate with an ***iambic trimetre*** *as in* **common** *or* **ballad metre**:

*"It **was** an **An**cient **Ma**ri**ner**
And he **stop**peth **one** of **three**
By thy **long** grey **beard** and **glit**tering **eye**
Now **where**fore **stop**pest thou **me**?"*

The Rime of the Ancient Mariner - Coleridge

This *metre* can be used **ironically** by poets when dealing with a serious subject, so watch out for a deliberate mismatch between the metre and the subject matter to make a point:

*"**What's** that **flut**tering **in** a **breeze**?
It's **just** a **piece** of **cloth**
That **brings** a **na**tion **to** its **knees**"*

Flag – John Agard

Sprung rhythm was coined by Gerard Manley Hopkins (1844-1889) for poetry where the rhythm depends on variable numbers of stressed and unstressed beats, believing that it more nearly imitated speech. In this, it is very close to *free verse*.

*No **wonder** of it: **sheer plod** makes **plough** down **sill**ion*
*__Shine__, and **blue-bleak embers, ah** my dear,*
*__Fall__, **gall** themselves, and **gash gold** vermilion."*

The Windhover – G M Hopkins

*"**Perch** on their **water-**perch **hung** in the **clear Bann** river*
*Near the **clay bank** in **al**der-dapple and **wa**ver, "*

Perch – Seamus Heaney

Two **syntactic** (*sentence formation*) **features** of poetry need to be understood as they are very important in seeing how poets vary *rhythm* and the effect of *rhyme.*

End-stopping is where the sense of the line, contained in a clause or sentence, ends at the end of the line, where the *metric line* ends:

"I stumbled in his hobnailed wake,"

This tends to emphasise *rhyme*, making it more insistent.

Enjambment is the opposite of *end-stopped.* The sense of the line continues onto the next line, often landing on a stressed beat, to emphasise the first word of the line, and enhance meaning:

*At the headrig, with a single **pluck***

*Of **reins**, the sweating team turned **round***
*And **back** into the land."*

Follower – Seamus Heaney

Heaney is using *enjambment* to *replicate* (copy) the movement
of the horses as they plough – up one line of the field, turning at
the top, and heading back down the field. Although *"round"*
syntactically makes sense as the end of a clause, the way one
says *"turned **round**"* gives an uplift in the voice, so leaves it
expecting a resolution, which comes in the next line with *"And
back"*. This is poetic genius.

Free verse is a modern form of poetry that has no regular
rhythm or *rhyme*. This is not to say that makes no use of either.
If there were neither rhythm nor rhyme throughout, then one
might as well call it prose, divided up into arbitrary lines. *Free
verse* frequently uses *enjambment* and *caesura* to guide the
reader through the argument and create rhythmic and rhyming
effects.

Printed in Great Britain
by Amazon